"When all cultures are visible, we can see ourselves as part of a community—sharing similarities and differences. Children learn this best by manipulating tangible items in their environment. Lisa Daly and Miriam Beloglovsky's creative vision and cultural research and Jenna's artful photos give us examples of how we can include cultural materials in our classrooms in meaningful ways, making this latest Loose Parts another valuable resource for us all."
　　—Joyce Daniels, MEd

"Words like *imaginative*, *creative*, *honoring*, *culturally appropriate* are beautiful placeholders for delving into *Loose Parts 3*. The book is a magical, joyful adventure in what can be created in early childhood environments. The photographs are like looking through a treasured family album, remembering our own delightful childhood play."
　　—Lorraine Lima, MA, Head Start consultant

"The Loose Parts series has quickly become an international phenomenon and has significantly shifted classroom practice for the good. These books have given early childhood educators inspiration and ideas that are immediately applicable in any setting and have a concrete way of connecting the intersection of theory-to-practice."
　　—Michelle Grant-Groves, EdM, author, advisor, and early education consultant

"Thank you, Lisa Daly and Miriam Beloglovsky, for having a vision that respects and elevates children's cultural identities. A century ago Maria Montessori told us the environment is the third teacher. *Loose Parts 3* brings twenty-first-century third teachers to the forefront and captures environments exceptionally well. Implicit in each page is relationship. Loose parts can act as a cultural broker for children and adults."
　　—Shawn M. Bryant, founding director and chief learning officer, Teaching Excellence Center

LOOSE PARTS 3

Other Redleaf Press Books by Lisa Daly and Miriam Beloglovsky

Early Learning Theories Made Visible
Loose Parts: Inspiring Play in Young Children
Loose Parts 2: Inspiring Play with Infants and Toddlers

Loose Parts 3

INSPIRING CULTURALLY SUSTAINABLE ENVIRONMENTS

Lisa Daly and Miriam Beloglovsky ■ Photography by Jenna Knight

Redleaf Press®
www.redleafpress.org
800-423-8309

Published by Redleaf Press
10 Yorkton Court
St. Paul, MN 55117
www.redleafpress.org

First edition 2018
Cover design by Jim Handrigan
Cover and interior photographs by Jenna Knight
Interior design by Erin Kirk New
Typeset in Berkeley Oldstyle and Trade Gothic
Printed in the United States of America

Library of Congress Cataloging-in-Publication Data

Names: Daly, Lisa, author. | Beloglovsky, Miriam, author.
Title: Loose parts 3 : inspiring culturally sustainable environments / Lisa
    Daly and Miriam Beloglovsky.
Other titles: Loose parts three
Description: First edition. | St. Paul, MN : Redleaf Press, 2018. | Includes
    bibliographical references.
Identifiers: LCCN 2017053657 (print) | LCCN 2018001731 (ebook) | ISBN
    9781605544670 (ebook) | ISBN 9781605544663 (pbk. : alk. paper)
Subjects: LCSH: Play. | Early childhood education—Activity programs. |
    Creative activities and seat work.
Classification: LCC LB1139.35.P55 (ebook) | LCC LB1139.35.P55 D36 2018
    (print) | DDC 372.21—dc23
LC record available at https://lccn.loc.gov/2017053657

Printed on acid-free paper   U18-07

To all who believe in equity

To all who advocate for social justice

To all who honor and value children's identities

To all who strive to understand and create culturally sustainable environments

To all who aspire to build relationships and create a sense of belonging

To all who desire to represent culture with authenticity, respect, and humanity

To all who seek authentic connections to real people and experiences

Contents

Acknowledgments

Part of our love for writing includes the opportunity to work with a wonderful group of colleagues, family members, friends, and students who support, inspire, and challenge us. Without them, our work would be harder and less rewarding. This book has been a powerful journey. We learned from each other and from many voices that validated and provoked our work and thinking.

We value the contributions of so many. Iris Dimond, thank you for your passion and relentless guidance, and for sharing your beautiful ceramic work with us. We are grateful to Jeanette Mulhern, Laurel Doyle, and Hannah Dimond for giving us their time and commitment to clean and design early childhood environments. To Eunyoung Hwang, we thank you for teaching us about your Korean culture and for sharing beautiful Korean artifacts and your amazing artistic abilities. Tim Craig, we are appreciative of our conversations and for the new knowledge and in-depth perspectives you shared. Cheri Quishenbery, we want to express thanks for all your support and assistance and acknowledge your reflective capacity and courage to do what is right for children. Denyse Cardoza and Gail Nadal, we thank you for your vision, leadership, and extraordinary support. We are indebted to Annette, Cassandra, Cheri, Jana, Josie, Leslie, Michael, Michelle, Sara, and Whitney for welcoming us into their learning environments and joining us in a culturally sustainable journey. Peggy at Asylum Down and Yabobo, thank you for opening your basement and for authentic baskets and instruments.

We want to acknowledge the contribution of our wonderful advisory members: Shawn Bryant, Kellie Cunningham Bliss, Joyce Daniels, Iris Dimond, Michelle Grant-Groves, Michael Leeman, Lorraine Lima, Cindy Linhares, Patrick Pieng, Tu Bears, and Esther Villa. We are forever grateful for your time, dedication, and wisdom. Our time together was powerful, moving, hard, and rewarding. You pushed us beyond our limits, revealed sticky issues, and provided valuable guidance. We look forward to our collaborative and significant work continuing and unfolding with deeper richness and delight.

Michelle Grant-Groves, you touch our hearts in so many ways. We want to give special recognition to you for being our reflective partner, asking the tough questions, and facilitating our advisory meetings. We are forever grateful to you for helping us articulate our design concepts. Thank you for being the change.

Jenna Knight, you give us hope for the next generation of educators. Your advocacy voice resonates loudly to shape the future of policy decisions that will positively impact young children and families and ensure that all children have access to high-quality education. Once again, your photography is inspiring and captures the vision of the manuscript.

We want to thank the staff at Redleaf Press for their ongoing support. David Heath, you are an incredible editor whose deep involvement strengthened the manuscript. Your encouragement means more than we can ever express. Laurie Herrmann, thank you for believing in us and for encouraging us. Kara Lomen, your wisdom continues to inspire us. Jim Handrigan, your cover design and creative direction on the interior have given us another beautiful book. Douglas Schmitz, we value your publishing insight and careful oversight of our manuscripts from start to finish. Sue Ostfield, your energy and ideas are remarkable. Eric Johnson, your marketing creativity is exceptional. Meredith Burks, we appreciate all you do to keep us informed. Steven Rhoden, we appreciate all your support and assistance.

Lisa: Words cannot express how grateful I am to Dan and Jenna for always being there and going the extra mile to help in every capacity throughout the writing and photographing of this manuscript. Thank you for your continued faithfulness, generosity, and support.

Miriam: For me this is a bittersweet book, because I wrote most of it as I supported my mom in her last days of life. I dedicate this book to her for always believing in me and for letting me know "Everything will work out, and you will be okay." Thank you, Mom and Dad.

Preface

We, the authors, have a vision of early childhood environments that not only support children's academic knowledge but also embrace and celebrate children's cultural identities. We believe that children deserve to learn in environments that are supportive of their identities. We want to inspire early childhood educators and families to empower children to engage in critical inquiry as they learn about people who are different from them.

Today's children need to be prepared to function in a not-yet-created world of the future, where they will have to successfully maneuver multiple global perspectives. Creativity and innovation as well as a global perspective are key skills that will be needed to be successful in the future. Children will need the skills to value, respect, and interact with a diverse group of people. In a constantly changing, diverse world, children must navigate multiple messages that either support or criticize their identities. Children's success can depend on how they use critical thinking to define their identities and define others around them. There is ongoing need for educational pedagogy that creates a sense of belonging, supports children's identities, brings joy and a sense of wonder, and is culturally responsive and sustainable. With that in mind, our goal for this book is to provide information that encourages educators to make a conscious and intentional effort to create culturally sustainable environments that allow children to grow to conquer a dynamic world. Culturally sustainable pedagogy affirms children's cultural identities and provides educators with a framework for creating equitable environments that reflect the culture, history, language, and traditions of the community.

In our journey as early childhood educators, we have learned that the multiuse and open-ended power of loose parts can promote cultural sustainability by embracing important cultural values, such as respect, integrity, and the core beliefs of every culture. Loose parts also support children to develop the critical and intellectual thinking to be successful in the undefined world of the future. We have made a conscientious commitment to use the loose parts educational philosophy as the lens to write this book. This book expresses our understanding of diversity, culture, and anti-bias education and how integrating a loose parts philosophy can support children's identities.

As educators, we can create environments that sustain the cultures of children and families entering early childhood programs. Our environments can be spaces that allow children to explore their identities as they play with loose parts. One of the most important values that we embrace is creating environments that promote a sense of wonder, curiosity, and joy. Our classrooms can be places where children and adults can join together in laughter and delight as they celebrate the joy of being their unique selves. In our journey researching the power of loose parts, we have seen that loose parts can also bring a sense of joy, curiosity, and wonder to children, families, and educators alike.

We also recognize that we do not always have all the answers and that instead we embrace the disequilibrium brought by ongoing discourse. We are constantly seeking new perspectives and are open to learning from our mentors, colleagues, and friends. We are willing to be vulnerable as we embrace diversity, and we recognize the challenges this brings.

Researchers Luis Moll, Cathy Amanti, Deborah Neff, and Norma Gonzalez (1992) coined the concept "funds of knowledge." These funds of knowledge are comprised of the stories of people as they interact in their daily life. Funds of knowledge are the histories of people and what they have learned through the generations in their families. We encourage you to engage as many funds of knowledge as are available within your diverse communities.

We hope that through this book, we can engage you in asking questions. We hope that you will join us in a quest for knowledge by continually seeking new perspectives that will enhance our collective work with young children and families. We hope that early childhood educators and families can work together to ensure that every child has a sense of belonging and opportunities to be who they are. We envision a future in which early childhood environments are designed to create hopeful futures for children, families, and educators.

Our Journey with Cultural Sustainability

As early childhood educators and advocates, we believe in the importance of valuing culture and diversity, including our own. We celebrate individual identities and acknowledge that as human beings, we have the talent, skills, abilities, and capacities to contribute to our family, community, and society at large. When we join together to share these differences, we can learn from each other and function in a cohesive, respectful, and responsible way, which allows us to communicate and share our culture, language, and heritage. We are cognizant of the power we hold as early childhood educators to teach children about the diverse world we live in. We want to expand children's knowledge about new languages, cultures, communities, and issues of social justice. Our desire for children's cultural education is one reason we decided to write a book on cultural sustainability.

As in all work that involves a deep study of diversity, as we wrote we confronted our own privilege and advantages in what seems to be an inequitable society. We considered the difference between equality (treating everyone the same) and equity, which takes differences into account. At one point during this ongoing reflection, we were challenged by our friend Michelle Grant-Groves with a powerful question: "How will you justify writing this book as two white women?" As we individually pondered this question, we explored our personal experiences, cultural values, personal history, and identity. We evaluated our past, upbringing, and biases and analyzed our role as allies and advocates for young children's rights to grow in a healthy, hopeful, and safe world. Our critical reflection led us to embrace the journey of writing this book, with passion and authenticity, and to develop a framework that informs our practice. The six concepts below serve as this book's framework for environmental design. For a more in-depth discussion of these concepts, see pages 11–18.

Aesthetics is the branch of philosophy that deals with the nature of art, beauty, and taste. It is a lens that allows us to look closely at the creation and appreciation of art, design, and beauty.

Authenticity is about being real and genuine, which is especially important in a cultural-learning space. Authenticity is what supports the exchanges between people that promote understanding, equity and equality, harmony, justice, and inclusion. Authentic interactions and environments allow us to learn from each other's history, individual experiences, traditions, values, and language, as they exist within our own individual cultural context. Authenticity helps us avoid stereotypical and biased assumptions.

Equity is not about treating all children the same. Instead, it is about achieving equal outcomes by individualizing support for each child. Educators need to recognize the inequities of practices that require every child to act the same way or create the same craft. Instead, they need to create environments that represent all children and promote equity and inclusive practices.

Dynamic means "always changing." We approach this concept from two different perspectives: (1) The nature of culture is dynamic. It shifts and changes with each group of children that enters the program. Cultural heritage is ever changing as communities grow and expand their knowledge. Even when heritage is sustained, there is still change as cultures adapt to a pluralistic society. (2) We also consider loose parts to be dynamic materials. The way children use loose parts is adaptable, flexible, and always different. The dynamic qualities of loose parts can support children's critical thinking and symbolic representation of their ideas and interests.

Praxis means "action informed by theory." Praxis is created as educators learn about the culture and language of the children in their program, and as they use this knowledge to guide their practices as they support children's identity, growth, and development. In other words, they put the theory into action.

Critical reflection is defined by us as the ongoing process of consideration, analysis, and informed decision making we apply to our daily work. We see critical reflection as a necessary skill for both educators and children. For educators, critical reflection helps us question our practices and thoughtfully and intentionally respond and support children's learning, development, and culture. Critical reflection is a crucial component of teaching and designing culturally sustainable environments.

Educational Influences

Many mentors and visionaries before us have sought to discuss the power of democratic environments and anti-bias education. We embrace the messages from wise leaders who have paved the way for all of us to create places that promote equity, safety, and joy for children. We invite you to learn more about the work of each of the following visionaries and mentors and to let their work guide your journey as educators into cultural sustainability.

Dr. Carol Brunson Phillips Day is recognized as a leader in early childhood education. She has served as president of the National Black Child Development Institute, as CEO and president of the Council for Professional Recognition, and on numerous boards and associations. Her ongoing advocacy for the rights of children has given us the power to unite our voices and engage in social justice. She encourages educators to promote cultural empowerment and to build environments that are culturally responsive. Cultural empowerment seeks to educate children within the context of their culture.

Lisa Delpit is a distinguished professor at Southern University School of Education and author of *Other People's Children: Cultural Conflict in the Classroom* (2006). She reminds us to always remember that children are individuals and cannot be made to fit into a preexisting mold. As educators, we need to recognize that we have to avoid the idea of creating a perfect environment for specific ethnic and cultural groups. Instead, we need to establish strong links and collaborations with families. She encourages us to join our collective spirit to solve racism and inequities and to create a world of justice and equity.

Louise Derman-Sparks, professor emeritus at Pacific Oaks College, is an author of many books on social justice. Her seminal work, the Anti-bias Curriculum (1989), has guided the early childhood profession not only to embrace culture but to reflect on the biases that interfere with and influence young children's identities. It has empowered educators to support children to engage in social justice work. The Anti-bias Curriculum offers values-based principles and methodology to develop and support higher critical thinking about issues of justice, equality, and inclusion. The four goals of the Anti-bias Curriculum have guided all our work with young children:

- Each child will demonstrate self-awareness, confidence, family pride, and positive social identities.
- Each child will express comfort and joy with human diversity; accurate language for human differences; and deep, caring human connections.
- Each child will increasingly recognize unfairness, have language to describe unfairness, and understand that unfairness hurts.
- Each child will demonstrate empowerment and the skills to act, with others or alone, against prejudice and/or discriminatory actions.

Julie Olsen Edwards is professor emeritus at Cabrillo College and author of many books and articles about issues of diversity and social justice. She collaborated with Louise Derman-Sparks to write *Anti-bias Education for Young Children and Ourselves* (2010). Anti-bias education has not only engaged the early childhood education community to explore the importance of honoring children and families, but it has taken us into the important work of social justice. Julie Olsen Edwards's deep compassion and commitment to justice and equity have inspired us to create spaces where children can thrive, families can have access to resources, and educators can be respected. She has awakened our desire to restore joy and wonder in early childhood education by advocating for the right of all children to be respected, celebrated, and honored.

Paolo Freire introduced us to the concept of education as a conversation instead of a curricular process. He stressed the idea that dialogue is not just about deepening understanding; it is part of making a difference in the world. He further emphasized the importance of a "pedagogy of the oppressed" (1968) and a "pedagogy of hope" (1992) as vehicles to promote awareness of inequalities, or conscientisize (to educate about an issue or idea) and influence reality. He argued that consciousness encourages the formation of critical consciousness, which allows people to question the nature of their historical and social situation.

Janet Gonzalez-Mena is a respected early childhood educator, professor, author, and trainer. In *Diversity in Early Care and Education: Honoring Differences* (2008), Gonzalez-Mena demonstrates her insightful and respectful views of culture. Her teachings are about understanding the cultural perspectives of families and how to incorporate these perspectives as we make decisions on the policies and practices we exercise as early childhood educators. She encourages us to listen and learn from each other's wisdom and experiences and to work together to create justice for families as they raise their children in a diverse world.

Zaretta Hammond's book *Culturally Responsive Teaching and the Brain* (2015) taught us that deep culture governs how we learn new information. For children to learn, they need to live in a space that acknowledges their identity and is free of elements and stereotypes that trigger an intense emotional charge. Hammond reminds us that the signs and symbols around us communicate with our collective unconscious mind. She addresses the importance of creating ethos, which reflects the specific defining character, sentiment, moral nature, or guiding beliefs of a person, group, or community. She invites us to use cultural values and convert them into concrete objects and symbols that create ethos in the classroom. This includes aesthetic values, rituals and routines, and everyday classroom traditions that support, respect, and embrace the culture of the children, families, and educators attending the program.

Dr. Gloria Ladson-Billings is a professor and vice chancellor at the University of Wisconsin and author of numerous articles and books. Her groundbreaking work in the fields of culturally relevant pedagogy and critical race theory served as inspiration and reflection as we wrote this book. She helped us understand the reasons for the educational disparity gap in our current educational system. Her strategies and the solid research outlined in her book *Dreamkeepers: Successful Teachers of African American Children* (1994) highlight the importance of focusing on children's culture as a source of strength and not a problem to be overcome or something completely invisible.

Dr. Leticia Nieto is a distinguished professor at St. Martin's University, author, dramatist, and psychotherapist. Her book *Beyond Inclusion and Beyond Empowerment* (2010) offered us a guide to attainable and sustainable social change in the contest of oppression. Her honest and compassionate approach to culture and diversity has opened our eyes to the importance of creating inclusive and culturally sustainable spaces that allow all voices to be heard and respected.

Dr. Sonia Nieto is professor emeritus at the University of Massachusetts in Amherst, an author, and a distinguished scholar. Her writings on the sociopolitical implications of culture and how they impact education have strengthened our desire to continue our work as child advocates. She encourages us to recognize that educators and students are deeply influenced, positively and negatively, by societal, educational, and ideological contexts. To lessen the achievement gap as early childhood educators, we have to find joy in diversity.

Vivian Gussin Paley is a respected early childhood educator and researcher who conducted most of her research at the University of Chicago Laboratory School. She is a recipient of a MacArthur Fellowship and has authored many books. Her work on story acting and storytelling as a way to make children's thinking visible has given us support to always promote the importance of play. She argues that observation leads to a deep knowledge of children's reality, language, and sociocultural context.

Dr. Patricia Ramsey is professor emeritus at Mount Holyoke College and an author. Her book *Teaching and Learning in a Diverse World: Multicultural Education for Young Children* (2004) taught us to go beyond the surface of culture to more deeply understand children and family values and children's early attitudes about gender, race, and socioeconomic class. We value her studies and writings.

We value the work of the **UNESCO Convention on the Rights of the Child** (1989), which follows two important concepts: the furtherance of the best interests of the child and nondiscrimination. UNESCO has advocated for children's right to education, regardless of their nationality, race, sex, or socio-economic status.

We are also indebted to **Luis Antonio Hernandez** for his commitment to bilin-gual/multicultural early childhood education. We are thankful for **Christina Lopez-Morgan** for fighting the good fight to support children, families, and early childhood educators and for her commitment to a bias-free and inclusive education. We embrace the teachings of **Brené Brown** on empa-thy and storytelling. We have learned from New Zealand's **Te Whāriki**, and the important work of integrating authentic culture into early childhood education.

This list is a small sample of the many influences in our combined sixty years as early childhood educators. We encourage you to explore their work and to seek out others who are supporting children's cultural development and learning in positive ways.

Theoretical Influences

Many theorists and educational philosophers have guided our work. For the sake of brevity, we focus on only four key theorists, but many other important schol-ars have influenced the cultural guidance of early childhood education.

John Dewey (1859–1952), in *My Pedagogic Creed* (1897), introduces the con-cept that education and learning only happen when the child is an active participant within the social consciousness of the family and the com-munity in which the child exists. At birth, children begin to interact with an environment that is continuously shaping who they are, the power they acquire, and the habits they develop. This active participation in a supportive environment begins to arouse children's ideas and feelings. This is how children in strong relationships with caring adults gradually come to share in intellectual and moral resources gathered together by the members of the community. Children are active participants in their own emotional well-being as well as active participants and contributing members of the society in which they live. Dewey argued that children are naturally curious and that they learn through thoughtful activities in well-provisioned environments. He said that children have strong instincts and these instincts are the foundations for learning. The environment plays a key role in connecting these instincts into real-life, meaningful experiences.

Jerome Bruner (1915–2016) believed that learning is an active process in which learners construct new ideas or concepts based on their prior knowledge and experience. He argued that human beings have a strong predisposition to culture and that children have an innate interest in the activities of their family and peers and try to imitate what they observe. He emphasized the importance of not just teaching children what to do but focusing on what children are thinking and the rationale behind that thinking. He introduced the idea of a cultural approach that allows children to gradually appreciate that they are not acting on "the world," but that their actions ultimately change the beliefs they hold about the world (Bruner 1996). This paradigm shift in children's understanding that they are acting based on their beliefs requires a shift in the approach educators take to ensure learning. For example, educators can recognize that children are capable of assuming more responsibility for their own learning and thinking. Educators can encourage inquiry that leads children to think more about their thinking. This is a concept known as metacognition, which is higher-level thinking that enables analysis of one's own learning or thinking processes. Bruner stressed that the outcomes of learning need to go beyond concepts, categories, and problem-solving techniques previously determined by the culture. Instead, he recognized that children have the ability to invent new things by themselves. His view of culture as an important part of the learning process has influenced educational pedagogy to be more responsive to the role of language and culture in children's learning and development.

Lev Vygotsky (1896–1934) argued that children thrive in an environment that promotes interactions with other adults and peers. Healthy cognitive and social-emotional development is fostered through these positive interactions and offers children a range of experiences. He discussed the relationship between thought, language, affect, and awareness, stressing that this can be best seen in the context of self-initiated, make-believe play. Vygotsky emphasized that learning that leads to changes in development happens when a child acquires specific cultural tools that are handed to them by more experienced members of their community. These cultural tools facilitate the acquisition of higher cognitive and social-emotional functions and take a different meaning depending on the culture from which they come. Cultural tools can be physical or abstract objects, such as a hammer, numbers, or letters. Or cultural tools can include ways of thinking and acting, such as using a language or averting eye contact. When children, educators, and parents provide cultural tools in the environment for children to accomplish different tasks, they become capable of acquiring higher-level thinking (Vygotsky 1978).

Urie Bronfenbrenner (1917–2005) is respected for his cross-cultural studies on families and their support systems and on human development and the status of children. He developed ecological systems theory to explain how everything in a child and the child's environment affects how a child grows and develops. Bronfenbrenner stressed the importance of studying children within the context of the multiple environments that influence their development. He viewed children as capable of influencing and shaping their world in social and cultural ways, which in turn nurtures their development. His ecological systems theory (Bronfenbrenner 1994) defined five different systems that impact the way children grow and develop:

- The **microsystem** is the most intimate, and it is comprised of the daily home, school, peer group, and community environments. In the microsystem, children engage in a personal back-and-forth exchange with family members, classmates, educators, and caregivers. This ongoing exchange influences children's developmental outcome.
- The **mesosystem** is the interaction between the microsystems—for example, the exchange that takes place between families and educators.
- The **exosystem** is comprised of people and places that affect the child's environment. These may include the family's workplace, extended family, government agencies, school boards, social services, and planning commissions.

- The **macrosystem** describes the culture in which individuals live. It includes ideologies, social expectations, legal and moral perspectives, traditions, and cultural values.

Voices of Advisers

We are indebted to the influential educators who have initiated the conversation about diversity and social justice. As we began to add our own voices as authors to the work, we realized that we needed advice, guidance, and support to ensure we were true to our values. We invited a diverse group of people who have a deep understanding of children and culture to form an advisory group. Our intent was to have representative voices that would bring cultural integrity and authenticity to our work. We wanted these advisers to evaluate, analyze, and affirm our core values and the messages in our photography. Below are some of the comments from our advisory group. We were validated, encouraged, and challenged by their comments on our work. (See the appendix for more information on the advisory group.)

Iris Dimond: "If there was ever any doubt about the validity and necessity for your work, please banish all of those thoughts and fears. You are compiling a powerful representation of culture and diversity in your learning environments."

Tu Bears: "Your gathering of photos and deep wisdom will fuel the lives of many hearts in our present day and for generations to come. Believe in your beautiful work and know that the cultures, diversity of humanity in our ONE planet are ready for the magic that is flowing from your rivers of knowledge."

Shawn Bryant: "In the words of Paulo Freire, 'Thank you for being vulnerable.' I personally thank you for modeling what cultural sustainability looks like in pictures. Thank you for making the inequitable equitable. Thank you for attempting to do what many people run away from. Thank you for confronting the discomfort."

Patrick Pieng: "Thank you so much for inviting us to participate in your journey. What you are aiming to accomplish is inspiring. I truly believe in your approach, in how you are obtaining feedback to strengthen the product you will be providing to the public. I definitely see how the influence of aesthetics, dynamism, and praxis are reflected in your photos."

Kellie Cunningham Bliss: "I leave feeling excited and rejuvenated. I loved the deep thinking, awareness, and respectfulness."

Michael Leeman: "I find the core values of 'authentic,' 'aesthetic,' and 'praxis' especially well represented in the photos."

Esther Villa: "Thank you for all the ideas you stimulated. The pictures are so inspiring, and I want to run home and get started on projects. What a special gift to the world!"

Joyce Daniels: "Your photos are thoughtfully taken and put together. Authentic: reflect many families. Aesthetic: beauty, inviting. Dynamic: invite both teacher and child to build, create, and change."

Lorraine Lima: "Your work is beautiful, valuable, and so relevant in these times. I appreciate your commitment to the field of study and to children and families."

Cindy Linhares: "I was inspired and grateful to have been a part of such an awesome think tank of professionals who have many common denominators and much passion for early childhood development. The discussions of race, ethnicity, diversity, what makes us individual and part of something bigger, and how we feel a sense of belonging really need to continue on a micro and macro level."

Michelle Grant-Groves (advisory group facilitator): "Bringing together a diverse group of educators to serve as advisers for Lisa and Miriam's upcoming book was an incredibly honoring experience. This group of dedicated professionals, wholeheartedly participated as a community of leaders to critically examine core elements of the book. All who participated brought with them a sense of honor, dignity, respect, and authenticity in their questions for the authors and each other. It is the advisory group's hope that readers of this book continuously seek to understand, inspire, and design culturally sustaining environments for young children in ways that reflect authentic connections to real people and real experiences."

We, as authors, are honored to have the voices of our colleagues and friends guiding our work. We have learned from each other, and we hope to represent our collective voices with accuracy and power. It is in unity that we grow in our respect and representation of our shared humanity. We will continue to engage in powerful conversations and in asking questions.

We have included a glossary of terms to deepen readers' understanding and knowledge of how loose parts inspire culturally sustainable environments. We hope you use the text and photography in this book as inspiration. Please adapt them to reflect the cultures and languages in your communities. We want you to create environments that reflect the ethos embraced by your own collective knowledge.

Programs Featured in This Book

The early care and education environments featured in this book are all located in California. This selection of programs may seem somewhat California-centric for readers who live elsewhere, but we purposefully photographed environments in the regions where we live and teach to have regular, ongoing, and accessible contact. Additionally, the programs are known to us and align with our core framework concepts—aesthetics, authenticity, equity, dynamic, praxis, and critical reflection. We identified environments that integrated the principles of cultural sustainability and followed a loose parts philosophy in a variety of diverse settings: center-based and family child care; Head Start, private, and parent cooperative; urban and rural; and coastal and Central Valley of California. We wanted programs that had long-standing traditions of supporting their children, educators, and families.

Some environments pictured are from programs with which we have a long relationship and the directors are our mentors. We also wanted to highlight programs that demonstrated a deep knowledge and understanding of the importance of play, sense of wonder, and joy to children and families. Our selection qualities and characteristics may undoubtedly describe your program. We wholeheartedly affirm that there are excellent, culturally sustainable early childhood programs throughout the United States that are inclusive, sensitive, and respectful. Selecting programs within our own communities gave us opportunity not only to photograph inspiring environments but to engage with educators and to have weekly reflective conversations. Being local allowed us to gain understanding of each program's cultural values and to have intentional dialogue with educators about how their classroom environments respectfully represent the cultures of children and families in their programs and communities. We joined programs in our community on a journey to affirm children's cultural identities and provide educators with a framework for creating equitable environments that reflect culture, history, language, and traditions of the community. We invite you to embark on the same journey in your own community.

These are the programs that appear in this book:

Center of Gravity in the San Francisco Bay Area cultivates children's natural
curiosity through the intentional teaching of Michelle Grant-Groves and her
staff. This STEM-based early childhood education lab school offers multiple
opportunities for children to re-create the world around them by exploring
complex relationships and connections. The educators endeavor to engage,
encourage, and empower all children (and families) to delight in and design
new possibilities in our world for the betterment of all people within our local
and global communities in the twenty-first century. The center fully embraces
the idea of cultural sustainability by providing a unique, inclusive space and a
place where creativity, community, and innovation are fostered for all children
and families in early childhood and beyond.

Cheri Quishenbery's Family Care outside of Sacramento, California, strives
to create an environment that is inviting, where children are challenged and
culture is celebrated. Cheri's ongoing critical reflection and creativity come
together as she designs and provisions her environment. Loose parts are used
in a dynamic way. She constantly challenges children to think and explore
their ideas. We value Cheri's advocacy and ability to support the importance
of going beyond stereotypes to create culturally sustainable environments.

Children's Circle Nursery School in Van Nuys, California, takes careful time
to transition one child at a time into their program. They encourage parents
to stay as long as five weeks when their child begins the program in order
to build a relationship between the child, family, and center. It is incredibly
comforting for parents when their child feels as if she belongs and trusts the
new adults in her life. An environment that is clearly designed to promote
a sense of trust requires intentionality and creativity. Tim Craig, the director of the program, carefully plans traditions with his staff that sustain the
children, families, and educators in the program. The environment creates a
strong sense of community that invites families to be who they are. Praxis is
used to validate the important work of honoring the children who attend the
program.

Loomis Head Start is in a rural area of California northeast of Sacramento and
part of KidzKount Head Start Agency. The program has an authentic and
aesthetic environment filled with loose parts that children manipulate daily.
Creativity abounds and the children engage in powerful conversations. The

diversity of families and educators is honored and respected, and the strength of each child is celebrated and embraced.

Roseville Community Preschool (RCP) is a parent-participation preschool that has abundant, intriguing, and engaging materials everywhere in the environment, both indoors and outdoors. Educators thoughtfully provision spaces for children to play, interact, problem solve, explore, and discover. Bev Bos, teacher, author, presenter, and our beloved mentor, was director of the program for over fifty years until she died in 2016. Bev was driven by her passion for play-based learning for preschoolers and touched the lives of everyone she met with her words of wisdom. Michael Leeman has taken over as the center's director and continues to advocate for play. He and the educators at RCP provide a child-centered program where children are free to enjoy childhood.

Folsom Lake College's Learning Environment and Cosumnes River College's Child Development Center were used to intentionally create our vision for a culturally sustainable environment combined with loose parts educational philosophy.

The Early Childhood Education Center at the University of California in Santa Barbara provides a beautiful environment that represents the local community with authenticity. The outdoor spaces are thoughtfully designed to incorporate native plants. The local artists have created aesthetic representations of the monarch butterflies that are native to the area.

While it is impossible to represent every child and every family, we hope that our work honors the voices of the children, families, and educators who are represented in this book. We want to give early childhood educators a voice that will encourage them to engage in this powerful and necessary work of creating culturally sustainable environments. We hope that readers will understand that it is impossible to give space to all diversity and that if we have excluded someone, it is not intentional. We invite you to reflect on your own community and to adapt the ideas in this book as you support children and families in your programs.

Part 1
An Introduction to Culturally Sustainable Environments

At younger and younger ages, children are negotiating difficult transitions between their home and educational settings, requiring an adaptation to two or more diverse sets of rules, values, expectations, and behaviors. Educational programs and families must respect and reinforce each other as they work together to achieve the greatest benefit for all children. For some young children, entering any new environment—including early childhood programs—can be intimidating.

—*Responding to Linguistic and Cultural Diversity Recommendations for Effective Early Childhood Education* (A position statement of the National Association for the Education of Young Children)

The ever-changing composition of early childhood programs is challenging early childhood educators to be more responsive to the diverse population of children they serve. Creating an environment that is culturally sustainable is imperative. Internationally renowned children's entertainer Raffi Cavoukian said, "If the young are not honored and respected for who they are, then they are going to grow up disenfranchised from their true authentic selves and are going to seek to connect in many, many afflicted ways" (interview for *The Third Teacher*, 2010).

Environments that embrace the cultural values of the children and families they serve demonstrate respect for the rights of all children to thrive, grow, and develop. Culture is created by the attitudes, customs, beliefs, and values shared by a group of people. It is transmitted from generation to generation through language, artifacts, music, daily rituals, and the arts. As children participate as members of the community, they are developing a strong sense of identity. This simple statement reminds us that as early childhood educators, we have the responsibility to offer children spaces that honor who they are and recognize their strengths as creative, curious, capable, caring, and competent human beings. Spaces that encourage play and promote a sense of wonder invite children to question and critically think about who they are in relationship to others, thus helping them develop their humanity.

Children's personality is shaped throughout their life span, and early success or failure affects later development. Children's identity develops from birth and continues through life. Early childhood is the time when children readily take initiative to accomplish things. This is a time when children need to express their ideas and thinking and begin to take ownership of who they are and what they want to do.

For children to gain a strong understanding of both self and group identity, it is important that educators establish a democratic classroom. Children have to be aware of others' points of view, balance their own needs with those of other members of the group, and negotiate and cooperate with a wide range of other individuals. Children develop these skills by practicing as they learn to connect with, learn from, and respect peers who are different from them. A culturally sustainable environment helps create inclusion, self-identity, empathy, and activism against injustice.

We believe that children and families have the right to attend programs that value who they are and support their contribution as strong members of the community. Loose parts environments that inspire hope and provide a sense of belonging have the attributes of enhancing children's learning and offering support and respite to families. Children and educators spend many hours a day in early childhood programs. These programs provide an intrinsic opportunity to integrate a loose parts philosophy that is important to children's lives and connects them to resources and experts in their community and culture. Loose parts are relevant to every child. They cross the boundaries of gender, age, abilities, and socioeconomic challenges.

We acknowledge that relationships are central in the development of culturally sustainable environments. As humans, we are all connected to nature, to culture, to our families, to food, and to our communities. We exist in close interdependence with one another. Understanding and nurturing these connections begins in early childhood, as children interact with the world they inhabit. These encounters inspire a sense of wonder and ongoing curiosity. For children to care for the world, from their own home to the homes of other children, they must first fall in love with the world they live in. When children find joy and wonder, they develop the foundation for empathy, stewardship, and responsibility. These are the qualities we need to promote in early childhood.

What Are Loose Parts?

The term *loose parts* was originally coined by British architect Simon Nicholson to describe open-ended materials that can be used and manipulated in different ways (Nicholson 1971). He believed that every human being has the potential to be creative. He also believed that loose parts in an environment invite immense imaginative possibilities unlikely in settings with fixed elements. An increasing number of early childhood classrooms are adopting the use of loose parts. Loose parts have the following characteristics:

- They can be made of many different materials, such as wood, metal, plastic, glass, fabric, or paper, or they can come from nature. Natural materials are available throughout the world and can be easily collected.
- They are open-ended, which means they can be used in a variety of ways.
- They are inviting and encourage children to use their senses to discover textures, sounds, smells, and colors.
- They are varied and can be sorted and classified.
- They can be recycled, repurposed, and upcycled.

We have come to recognize loose parts as an educational philosophy that supports children's development and learning. Loose parts can help children do the following:

- connect to nature and their local environment
- gain autonomy as they invent and act on specific ideas about how loose parts should be used
- increase their knowledge of the world around them
- develop creativity and musical and artistic expression
- solve problems creatively
- use inquiry to test ideas and hypotheses
- build self-awareness and self-confidence
- increase their ability to find similarities and differences through classification
- learn about their responsibility to care for and preserve the environment for today and the future
- engage their sense of wonder and curiosity as they explore the world
- develop divergent thinking
- collaborate and negotiate with peers and adults

Loose parts promote a variety of play and learning opportunities. Consider the following examples and stories of children playing with loose parts.

. . . .

Four-year-old Chen uses colorful crystal beads and pretends to mix them in a wok. She uses her grasping skills as she manipulates a set of bamboo tongs. She then takes paper squares and crumbles them into the bamboo steamer. She is preparing a meal of vegetables and dumplings for her friends Louis and Erika.

. . . .

Angel begins to bang on a variety of pots and pans that families brought into the program. He then arranges some wooden bowls and cardboard boxes and listens as he bangs on them. He experiments with different sounds by using metal and wooden utensils. He demonstrates the different sounds to Marena, who is sitting next to him. He tells her, "This is how my dad drums when we go to my family." Angel is a member of the Miwok community, where drumming is part of their gatherings and ceremonies. Joaquin joins in and starts singing a familiar song in his home language, Spanish. He continues to bang as he sings a popular children's song: "Pin Pon es un muñeco muy guapo y de cartón . . ." ("Pin Pon is a beautiful doll made of cardboard"). Other children join in, and they learn about each other's cultures.

. . . .

When provided with a variety of colorful tiles, Erik notices that they have designs similar to some of the ceramic dishes they use in his house. He then proceeds to arrange the tiles in a variety of combinations. The educators notice his intent and ask his family to bring in some ceramics the children can use as inspiration. This leads into an exploration of ceramics from around the world.

. . . .

Mariano, twenty-four months, takes a piece of fabric and gathers some colorful paper and colorful stones. He rolls the paper and stones into the fabric and exclaims, "Yum, burrito." Mariano's family is from the state of Sinaloa in Mexico, where burritos are common. He is using loose parts to symbolically represent food that he has eaten in his own cultural experience.

. . . .

Aki's grandmother, who is Japanese, showed the children how to use a scarf to create a bag they can use to carry loose parts. The children became interested and wanted to learn more about the ancient Japanese art of furoshiki, which is a traditional Japanese wrapping cloth that is used as a bag for carrying items. The children were excited, and this moment led to a conversation about not using plastic bags when going to the market. By exploring the ancient art of furoshiki, children are not only learning about Japanese culture, but are making an important connection to eco-friendly ways to sustain the environment for future generations.

As you may notice in the children's stories so far, cultural interactions are a part of daily life, as are loose parts. Integrating loose parts can support children's development in a culturally sustainable environment.

What Is a Culturally Sustainable Environment?

Children today live in a diverse world where they participate in social interactions that may be unfamiliar to them. This is particularly true when children's cultures are different than the cultures of the majority of children and adults around them. In her seminal article "Toward a Theory of Culturally Relevant Pedagogy," Gloria Ladson-Billings (1995) highlights the importance of creating pedagogy that is relevant to children's culture and language. She stresses that "culturally relevant pedagogy must provide a way for students to maintain their cultural integrity while succeeding academically" (476).

So what is *cultural sustainability*? The concept is fairly new. It originated from the idea that through validating our culture, history, language, traditions, and environment, we can meet the needs of the present without compromising the needs of future generations. When we embrace cultural sustainability in our classrooms, we have to reflect on culture—both our own and others'. *Culture* is a word that has many different meanings. When we talk about culture in this book, we mean the deep values shared by a group of people. Each of us has a culture that provides us with a sense of place and belonging. Our culture encompasses our history, heritage, language, celebrations, values, and traditions. Culture shapes our identity and the way we experience the world. It helps us make connections and build relationships that sustain us and build our humanity. As early childhood educators reflect on their own cultures, they learn to value the cultural identity of the children and families in their program.

Sustainability is based on the premise that all parts of a system are interdependent, and they do not function individually. Sustainability requires education that fosters empathy, caring, and responsible citizenship. Early childhood educators are in a position to help children learn the values, attitudes, and skills they need to embrace a mind-set of sustainability, especially when it comes to cultural sustainability.

Culturally sustainable pedagogy raises children's awareness about what it means to belong to a specific culture and community. Culturally sustainable pedagogy considers children's feelings, beliefs, thinking, history, and behaviors. When we teach with cultural sustainability in mind, we focus on children's strengths and do not expect children to give up their identities in order to blend into mainstream societal expectations. Instead, we support children in gaining power in their cultural knowledge and strengths to be successful in a pluralistic world. In a culturally sustainable environment, children's personal and group identities are respected, while children learn to respect the diverse identities of others.

For children to thrive in an early childhood environment, educators need to be responsive to the children's culture, language, and heritage. To create a culturally sustainable environment that supports children's identity and sense of belonging, think about incorporating opportunities for children to do the following:

- learn about each other and respect differences
- develop compassion
- value the social and cultural contributions of others
- broaden creative (divergent) and critical (convergent) thinking skills
- demonstrate compassion and empathy
- experience fairness and equity
- feel valued and respected
- speak up against unfairness
- work toward a common goal
- explore their identity and the identities of others

It is the responsibility of early childhood educators to create indoor and outdoor environments that let children know they belong and are valued. It is also important for early childhood educators to embrace their own culture and language and to build a healthy interdependence with other members of the community. Culturally sustainable environments empower children to think critically as they share their ideas and actively participate in decision making. A culturally sustainable environment acknowledges and invites children's cultures to help them make meaning and understand the world they inhabit.

As the cultural diversity of children entering early childhood environments continues to expand, it is imperative that as a profession we move from just teaching facts and memorization skills to a more holistic approach that encourages children to interact positively with one another. In a report on education for sustainable development, UNESCO introduced four pillars of learning and intercultural education (Woodhead 2006):

- learning to know
- learning to do
- living together
- learning to be

Cultural sustainability supports each of these pillars of education in the following ways.

Learning to Know

Culturally sustaining environments promote lifelong learning through in-depth investigations and explorations that allow children to seek and find answers. During this process, they will come across different languages, areas of knowledge, and cultural values. Through these interactions, children can increase their ability to find knowledge and interact with a diverse group of people and perspectives while preserving their own.

Learning to Do

Culturally sustaining environments are provisioned to engage children in multiple opportunities to problem solve, think critically, deal with many situations, and work in collaboration. Children need to learn about local and global perspectives in order to acquire the skills to find a place in society.

Living Together

Culturally sustaining environments help children develop an understanding of other people's history, traditions, and spiritual values. Children need to gain a healthy interdependence as they work on joint projects and manage conflict. These interactions need to be in the spirit of respect for the values of pluralism, mutual understanding, and cultural diversity.

Learning to Be

Culturally sustaining environments view each child as capable and competent, with respect for children's cultural and language potential. Early childhood environments need to support and promote individual children's identity and personality and foster a sense of personal meaning. They need to offer children opportunities to act with greater autonomy since they are respected and valued as fully functioning social, emotional, and cognitive human beings.

Loose Parts Can Support a Culturally Sustainable Environment

Loose parts are materials that clearly represent and embrace the diverse culture found in early childhood environments. Young children may use loose parts in multiple ways, but they are substantially more than open-ended objects. They are part of an educational philosophy educators can embrace for their power to transform early childhood learning environments and provoke meaningful play experiences. The open-ended qualities of the loose parts allow children to re-create and represent their cultures and home languages in a variety of ways. Within culturally sustainable pedagogy, loose parts increase the thinking possibilities for young children as they gain power over their own capacities. Combining loose parts with culturally sustaining pedagogy can support children's development and learning in the following ways.

Learning through Symbolic Play

Because loose parts lend themselves to be manipulated in a variety of ways, they may support the development of symbolic play. When children play "cooking" by using loose parts (such as stones, beads, and pots and dishes from their culture), they are learning that there are specific social rules that are required when working together in the kitchen. They learn that each culture may use different tools and utensils to achieve the preparation of food. And they may begin to represent those behaviors and tools symbolically through loose parts.

The ability to acquire abstract thinking is an important developmental process that is promoted through make-believe play. Loose parts support symbolic play and may increase children's ability to separate the object from the symbol. For example, children may use fabric as a superhero cape and pretend to fly. They probably know that the fabric does not have superhero power, but they can still pretend that it does.

Learning about Each Other and Respecting Differences

Early childhood environments that reflect the diversity of the community can support children in learning about different points of view, cultures, languages, and traditions. Because loose parts are open-ended and are free of biases and stereotypes, all children can interact with them equally, without any preloaded ideas of how they ought to be used.

Creative (Divergent) and Critical (Convergent) Thinking Skills

Creative (divergent) thinking and critical (convergent) thinking are essential to the process of learning, to assessing what we learn, and to functioning in a global society. Loose parts provide children opportunities to develop both types of thinking, since they can freely manipulate and change what they do with the loose parts. When children develop critical and divergent thinking and can generate ideas about differences and similarities, they gain appreciation for diversity and can engage in social justice work. In other words, the more children play with loose parts, the more they may develop the thinking skills that will help them understand differences and similarities and engage in the process of positive societal change.

Growing toward Equality and Equity

When children use critical thinking to question unfairness, they are actively participating in "the practice of freedom; the means by which men and women deal critically and creatively with reality and discover how to participate in the transformation of their world" (Freire 1994). Louise Derman-Sparks (1989) says that the "practice of freedom" is fundamental to promoting goals that enable every child to do the following:

- construct a knowledgeable, confident self-identity
- develop comfortable, empathetic, and just interactions with diversity
- develop critical thinking and the skills for standing up for oneself and others in the face of injustice

Critical thinking empowers children to fully participate in creating environments that promote equality and equity.

Developing and Demonstrating Empathy

Empathy is an essential trait that helps us make meaningful connections with others in both our work and personal lives. Empathy requires the ability to suspend judgment and to listen and understand another person's feelings. In our work with loose parts, we have noticed that the open-ended nature of loose parts gives children opportunities to play cooperatively. They take on other people's roles and invite other children to join as they take turns pretending to be a mother or father, using fabric as articles of clothing. Taking others' roles allows young children to see different perspectives. Thus, they begin to develop a better understanding of other people's thinking and to respond with empathy.

Supporting Children's Strengths

Children are capable and competent, and they are driven by an intense sense of curiosity. Children deserve caring adults who focus on their strengths and allow them to test their knowledge and skills. Educators can build on children's strengths by infusing loose parts into the environment and giving children time to freely explore the loose parts and test different ideas. When you observe children as they create a complex structure using loose parts, it is obvious that they are thinking, concentrating, creating, and using their imagination. There is a sense of accomplishment when they complete a task. When children feel competent, they are more willing to take initiative, be resourceful, ask questions, work together, and listen to different points of view. These are some of the same qualities children bring to make a difference in schools and communities.

Promoting Democracy

A community that supports children's strengths and includes every child is setting the foundation for participatory democracy. When educators create environments that respect children's cultures and language, children feel free to express themselves and fully participate in a democratic process. Loose parts involve children directly in making decisions, testing ideas, and sharing their experiences with other children. As they are playing with loose parts, children engage in participatory democracy, which can also be understood as a mode of being in the world, as a form of living together. Loose parts play maximizes these important skills and abilities needed to interact with other people and be a successful citizen of a democratic society.

Assuming Responsibility for the Environment

Because loose parts are often recycled or upcycled items, they can support ecological sustainability and teach children the responsibility to maintain future environments. Children can participate in their communities by collecting and preserving loose parts. Children can learn that you don't always need to purchase items. Instead, you can actively participate and understand that recycling helps sustain the environment and preserve it for future generations. When children participate in recycling and repurposing loose parts, they assume responsibility to maintain their environment for the present and future generations. This is one of the important concepts of a culturally sustainable environment.

Supporting Use of Home Languages and Cultural Values

Culturally sustaining environments support children's linguistic and cultural identities. Loose parts can be incorporated into the environment to engage children in using their own linguistic and cultural capacities as they build, role-play, and use loose parts in art. In her landmark research on culturally sustainable pedagogy, Gloria Ladson-Billings (1995) argues that to create equality and equity in education, we need to produce students who can achieve academically, are culturally competent in their own culture, and understand and critically question societal rules and norms. She stresses the importance of supporting children's community and cultural heritage by maintaining their language and other cultural practices.

Creating Culturally Sustainable Environments

When we design culturally sustainable environments, we consider six important core ideas:

- **aesthetics**, which influence children's appreciation for beauty and the arts
- **authenticity**, which is how children's history, values, and traditions are represented in the environment
- **equity**, which is the process of ensuring that all children have access to early childhood environments that represent who they are and recognize and support their strengths, culture, language, and heritage
- **dynamic**, which is the nature of culture and can describe the way children use loose parts, influencing children's development and learning
- **praxis**, which is using theory to lead our actions as we respond to children's culture, language, and values
- **critical reflection**, which guides us to observe, question, and respond to children's ideas and thinking

Aesthetics

Aesthetics deal with the nature of art, beauty, and taste. Focusing on aesthetics allows us to create and appreciate art, design, and beauty. According to Abraham Maslow (1999), humans have an inherent need for aesthetics, which he considered to be an integral part of the human experience.

An aesthetically pleasing environment can promote children's creativity and artistic expression. It can also connect children to the aesthetic values of their culture. Thoughtful, well provisioned, and aesthetically pleasing spaces encourage children to care and participate more actively in a community of learners. When children spend their days in an environment that is beautifully designed, they have the opportunity to thrive and learn to trust. Every culture has a powerful artistic contribution, and children have the ability to embrace the aesthetic values of diverse cultures.

AESTHETICS IN YOUR CULTURALLY SUSTAINABLE CLASSROOM ENVIRONMENT

The elements of design—symmetry, balance, color, texture, style, form, contrast, and space—provide the foundation to build an aesthetically pleasing and culturally sustainable environment. Using plants and natural materials to enhance and delineate specific areas adds warmth. Draped fabrics create seclusion and add interest and texture to the environment. Light and shadows add intrigue to specific spaces. Cushions, rugs, carpets, and blankets soften the environment. Mirrors placed in strategic spaces give the illusion that the room is bigger than it is. Thoughtfully selected colors can change the ambiance to reflect the children's moods. You should avoid using commercial materials and photographs that do not represent the diversity of the world in which we live. Instead, strive to represent the children and families in the program.

SELECTING AESTHETIC LOOSE PARTS

Integrate loose parts that reflect diverse cultures, stimulate children's senses, and allow children's innate aesthetic values to emerge. Sound gardens, created with familiar loose parts, add interest and offer children the opportunity to play with music and rhythm. Providing colorful tiles inspires children to design and express their feelings and ideas. Beautiful, natural jacaranda pods and ayoyote seeds used in musical instruments stimulate children's auditory sense. Mortars and pestles can be used to grind spices. The aromas stimulate children's sense of smell and sustain their memories of familiar smells. Mud cloth, or bogolan, is a cotton fabric made in Mali using a traditional process of dying with fermented mud. These fabrics can inspire children's art. To further enhance their creativity, add shells, strings, ribbons, pebbles, and buttons. Mud cloth is part of the Malian identity, and each piece uses different symbols to tell a story.

Authenticity

Authenticity is the quality of being genuine, traditional, and realistic. When we create and support authentic environments for children, we learn about children's histories, individual experiences, traditions, values, and languages. Through these powerful exchanges, we are transformed and come together to share what is meaningful and authentic to educators, children, families, and the greater community. For example, it is important to recognize that diversity exists within cultural groups and that people from the same ethnic background experience their culture in different ways. For instance, not all Mexican people avoid eye contact. Some people in Mexico may not look you in the eye, but other people make full eye contact. These cultural values are based on the individual lived experiences, which are influenced by factors such as geography, age, religion, and socioeconomic status.

Therefore, it is crucial to avoid overgeneralizations and stereotypes when creating opportunities for children to explore their individual cultures. Offering facts and cultural dates to children is not enough. It is important to engage them in critical thinking about their own culture and how they can make deep connections with other children in the program. Educators must build on children's life experiences and consistently bring these experiences into the classroom. Current and relevant life examples engage children in deeper learning and help them make connections with their individual, community, national, and global identities. When we value cultural authenticity, children, families, and educators develop strong relationships based on understanding of each individual's unique identity. When environments are authentic and free of stereotypes, we affirm each child's culture, ethnicity, gender, abilities, and spirituality.

AUTHENTICITY IN YOUR CULTURALLY SUSTAINABLE CLASSROOM ENVIRONMENT

Imagine an early childhood classroom where the educators, children, and families learn together in an environment that facilitates a deep level of sharing about their culture, language, history, and traditions. This type of environment is created through cultural authenticity. Start by designing an environment that supports and promotes cultural sustainability. Research the history and resources available in your local community. Talk to families, community members, and other people who belong to the diverse countries and cultures you work with. Represent diversity accurately and without stereotypes.

Ensure that the loose parts placed in the environment are authentic representations of items found in children's homes and not stereotypical "tourist approach" items bought in educational stores. Represent culture with authenticity and with respect and celebration of humanity. Learn about the culture, language, and traditions of children and families in your classroom, and select loose parts that represent and sustain their culture. For instance, add a pretty tablecloth and include a wide variety of items from home, such as Mexican ceramic cups or Korean tableware, when you design an imaginative play space. Such staging helps children feel comfortable around things that were previously foreign. Add cooking utensils from different parts of the world that children can use in imaginative play or in the sandbox. Offer children fabrics from around the world to use as costumes or as inspiration to design or create works of art.

Equity

There is no single best interpretation of equity. For the purpose of our work and as part of our framework, we define equity as the process of ensuring that all children have access to early childhood environments that represent who they are and recognize and support their strengths, culture, language, and heritage. Equity is not about treating all children the same. Instead, it is about achieving equal outcomes by individualizing support for each child. Equity is achieved when differences are acknowledged and similarities are celebrated. Equity involves planning everyday interactions and explorations with children, families, and community members. Equity is achieved when all children receive the resources they need, regardless of factors such as race, gender, sexual orientation, ethnic background, English proficiency, immigration status, socioeconomic status, and disability.

Helping children uncover difference and diversity in a supportive environment has the potential to transform future societies and increase acceptance and respect for others. Through equity, all children will have the knowledge and skills to succeed as contributing members of a rapidly changing, global society. By giving every child a positive start in life, we are setting the stage for future success.

Children enter early childhood programs with diverse needs and approaches to learning, and different cultural values and languages. Robinson and Jones-Diaz (2005) argue that early childhood programs that include concepts of equity and social justice are key in maximizing children's potential and learning. The United Nations Convention on the Rights of the Child encourages children's rights and contends that equity and diversity need to be fully integrated in educational, governmental, and social policy (Woodhead 2006). Focusing on equity and diversity acknowledges that children have different life experiences. Equitable environments respond to children's interests and include spaces that allow children to express their knowledge and thinking. Because culture is dynamic, our early childhood environments should change as children shift their understanding of the world and develop new knowledge and interests.

Dynamic

Culture is dynamic. It shifts and changes with each group of children that enters the program and as communities grow. We also consider loose parts to be dynamic because they offer children open-ended opportunities to represent their ideas and thinking.

Because culture is dynamic, it requires flexibility and adaptability, which children gain as they play with dynamic loose parts. Children's connection to their culture develops through warm and secure relationships. When children feel secure within the context of their culture, they in turn learn to respect the cultural values of other people. Because loose parts are naturally dynamic, they encourage children to take calculated risks and engage in testing unfamiliar items and spaces. The ever-changing power of loose parts offers children the opportunity to explore their daily reality.

An environment that is designed to support the dynamic nature of both culture and loose parts may sustain the language, art, cultural traditions, heritage, and values of children and families in the program. Observe and listen to children's play with loose parts. Notice how they negotiate and share their daily experiences with each other. Support their interest and embrace the change that comes from the dynamic exchange and interactions between children.

Selecting dynamic loose parts is easy to achieve, since children use their imagination to manipulate the loose parts in different ways. Loose parts provide children with multiple opportunities to explore, invent, and create their own reality. To deepen children's knowledge of other cultures, look for loose parts from different countries. Use the concept of *less is more*, and add a few types of loose parts at a time; however, make sure that there are plenty of the same loose parts. This gives children the opportunity to fully explore the possibilities of each item.

Praxis: From Theory to Practice

Praxis means combining our theories with our practical applications. Praxis combines child development theory with practical applications and experiential learning. To create praxis, educators have to engage in ongoing reflection about what works and what we need to change in our work. When educators take the time to reflect on their biases, assumptions, and stereotypical thinking, they are able to implement practices that embrace moral and ethical values and beliefs. Combining theories into our work requires a commitment to human well-being, the search for truth, and respect for others.

With regard to cultural sustainability, praxis means creating environments that embrace the cultural and linguistic capacities of every child in the classroom. Our job is to build on the knowledge and strengths of the children in order to validate their cultural identities.

SELECTING LOOSE PARTS THAT PROMOTE PRAXIS

Observe children as they play with loose parts. Think of what you see and what you learn from their play. What are their interests? What are they attempting to figure out? As you assess and develop a hypothesis about the children's intent, you can better support their learning. For instance, when children spend time in pretend cooking, you can use your observations and knowledge of the children's culture to intentionally add loose parts into the environment to further support their play.

Critical Reflection

Critical reflection is the act of stepping back, taking time to analyze, and asking probing questions that lead to change. When educators engage in critical reflection, they can thoughtfully and intentionally respond and support children's learning, development, and culture. John Dewey (1938) defines reflection as the act of creating a mental space in which to contemplate a question or idea, such as the following:

- What do I know now about young children?
- What do I know about myself, as a teacher of young children?
- What assumptions might I be making about children's culture?

Critical reflection allows us to question our practices and makes thinking visible. It helps us bring light to our deep, thoughtful, and intentional work with children.

CRITICAL REFLECTION IN YOUR CULTURALLY SUSTAINABLE CLASSROOM ENVIRONMENT

Critical reflection requires taking a risk and engaging in discourse that may not always be comfortable. It is within this risk that we can learn from each other and embrace conversations that lead to equity and fairness. When designing culturally sustainable environments, it is important to spend time reflecting on our biases and our cultural assumptions. Question your decisions, and listen to different perspectives. Critical reflection helps develop goals and guiding principles to apply in your roles as an educator. As authors, we constantly stop to reflect and ask, How are culture, gender, abilities, and family constellations of the children and families represented in this book? Are we introducing authentic images, tools, and loose parts into the environment? When we have doubts, we reflect with a member of the specific culture or invite our advisory members to give us feedback. We reflect on our own assumptions and biases and question our purpose. Each photo you see in this book was taken after a critically reflective process. We hope that you, too, will engage in critical reflection as you design culturally sustainable early childhood environments.

SELECTING LOOSE PARTS USING CRITICAL REFLECTION

When you select loose parts for an environment, start with a critical reflection process. These are some of the questions to ask when considering types of loose parts:

- What will the children do with the loose parts? For example, will they use the loose parts to engage in conversation about their feelings and ideas?
- Are the loose parts responsive to and representative of children's culture? Listen to children's conversations as they describe the loose parts. Observe if they seem to be familiar with the objects and how they use them in symbolic play.
- Do the loose parts help promote respect for self and others? Observe and document the collaboration between children as they explore loose parts together.
- Do the loose parts invite children to explore their identities in positive and growth-promoting ways? Notice how the children describe themselves as they match paint chips and ceramic pieces to their skin color.
- Do the loose parts offer children a global perspective? Listen to see how children make connection to loose parts from other countries. Are they able to make connection to loose parts with which they are familiar?

We encourage you to develop your own set of questions to guide your practices. We also invite you to observe, listen, and learn along with the children and families in your program. They have a wealth of information and knowledge to help you design your culturally sustainable environment.

These words serve as the framework for our design work and as a guide in the writing of this book. We hope that you consider these powerful words as you design early childhood environments that are responsive to children's culture, language, and values.

The Role of the Early Childhood Educator

Early childhood educators are in the privileged position to influence children's perspectives and learning. This requires commitment, education, reflection, creativity, and intentionality. Intentionality and creativity are necessary dispositions when creating spaces that are joyful, promote wonder, are inclusive, and reflect the lives of the children, families, and educators in the program. To recognize the value of children's identities, it is important for early childhood educators to critically recognize and analyze our own individual differences and find joy in our identities. Your identity defines who you are. Identity represents your interests, history, traditions, relationships, and social interactions.

Finding your identity may be a struggle as you ask yourself, Who am I? or Who do others want me to be? You can begin by exploring your own cultural identities and by researching your family history and traditions. Consider what messages you received growing up that influence what you believe about children. Did you grow up in an environment where independence was encouraged, or did you have to follow instructions and listen to the adult's guidance and requests? Consider how these messages will influence your environments and the way you guide children. Analyze how your own beliefs are similar to or different from those of the families in the program.

Design Environments to Support Children's Identities

To support children's identities, the environment needs to be welcoming and create a sense of belonging. All children need to see themselves represented in the environment. They need to know that they are valued and supported. This means that there is intent and purpose for every loose part, artifact, exploration, and material that is integrated into the environment.

Offer children loose parts and tools that allow them to gain competence in a hands-on, practical, and interactive way. Consider loose parts that encourage children to explore different perspectives, to use their home language, to engage in collaboration, and to increase their social and cultural heritage.

Design Environments That Support a Sense of Being

The concept of *being* requires educators to be present and in the moment. To be in the here and now honors children's right to experience the joy of childhood. When children explore mirrors, they discuss their personal attributes. For example, they may notice that all children have eyes, but they vary in color. As they build with blocks and large boxes, they may recognize that both girls and boys have the strength and power to build and construct large structures. Being is linked to identity. It involves children developing awareness of their culture, history, heritage, and traditions and children's importance in their world. When setting explorations for young children, consider offering possibilities for children that answer questions such as these:

- Who I am?
- How do I belong?
- How do I influence my community?

Design Environments That Create a Sense of Belonging

People have a natural need to belong to a group and culture and to be a valued member of society. Creating a sense of belonging requires dedication, knowledge, time, and effort. It is important that early childhood educators recognize that young children are egocentric, and that they make every learning opportunity personal. Children begin their explorations by first focusing on themselves, and then they extend their knowledge to others. At first they have a hard time meeting the idea that the same attribute can belong to many groups. Educators can support children in getting a strong sense of group identity by introducing the concept of "family."

Encourage children to discover specific characteristics that are found in their family—for example, the color of their eyes, the color of their hair, and so on. After children make a connection with the concept of belonging to a family, they can expand their thinking into belonging to other ethnic, cultural. or racial groups.

Design Environments That Support Diversity

Promote a classroom where every child can flourish and learn about diverse cultural values, and where every family participates as active members of the community. Exploring language in a variety of ways affirms children's own culture and invites them to explore the culture of other children in the classroom. At a parent meeting, invite families to work together on a family collage. This promotes a sense of community and allows children and families to connect through their similarities and respect their differences. Displays of different games, such as mancala, tangrams, marbles, and homemade games, can be placed in the environment as a way for children to connect with the concept that there are a variety of games people play in different parts of the world.

As children mature, they begin to develop self-awareness. Through the use of the language and visual arts, they begin to represent their thinking in a symbolic way. Young children also begin to classify and make sense of objects and events in their world. This process allows them to imagine and act out other people's perspectives. This is how children acquire the concepts of equity, justice, and inclusion. Through art, music, dramatic play, and storytelling, children express their social, linguistic, and cultural identities. They then begin to expand their capacity to develop the mutually respectful relationships essential for them to live responsibly in a diverse world (Derman-Sparks and Edwards 2010). An environment that has many representations and artifacts of the children's cultural background supports their capacity to respect a diverse group of people.

Music and instruments from different parts of the world give children a global perspective and introduce them to rhythms and styles that support their musical appreciation. Construct a sound garden outside where children can make and listen to different types of sound created by household items. It is amazing how these simple things promote powerful conversations among children.

· · · · · · · · · · · · · · · · · · · ·

At group meeting time, Javon shares that he wants to play the drums, but his mom cannot afford them. Later that day, Javon, Diego, and Camilla test the wind chimes, gong, pots, and pans in the sound garden. Camilla says to Javon, "Maybe we can make a set of drums for you to take home. See, we can use pots and pans." Camilla's interest in making a set for Javon demonstrates her respect for him.

Consider children with diverse abilities when selecting loose parts. For example, you can introduce letters and other loose parts made out of corrugated cardboard to engage children who have limited vision or are visually impaired.

Design Environments That Build Empathy and Care for Self and Others

Empathy is the ability to recognize, appreciate, and respond to another's feelings. Empathy is an important part of learning to get along with others. Set opportunities for children to play with each other, such as a loose parts collaborative project. Offer multiple opportunities for children to role-play different characters as they engage in symbolic play. When children actively engage in role playing, they begin to understand one another's thinking and perspectives. Use loose parts to create small worlds. Small-world play is an imaginative play experience that involves miniature environments for children to use in storytelling. Using persona dolls is another effective approach for discussing feelings, taking care of each other, and promoting empathy.

Design Environments That Promote Healthy Interactions

We urge educators to take the time to consider how racism, ableism, ageism, heterosexism, religious and faith biases, and classism affect young children. Include books representing a wide diversity of people, including gay, lesbian, and transgender families. When children walk in the center, consider having their photographs mounted on small wood blocks so that they can move their photo from the "home" basket to the "school" basket as a routine for signing in. This gives them a visual representation of who is at school and invites them to sort and classify differences and similarities. They can also place their mounted photos to let other children know they are still working on an art project or a block structure. The mounted photographs become loose parts they can use in their play. The conversations can become rich with descriptions, such as this one:

· · · · · · · · · · · · · · · · ·

As Diego starts to move his photo to the "I am here basket," he says, "Look, Mom, my eyes are darker than Javon's." He continues to look at all the photos and exclaims, "Alonzo is here, and he is different than me, but I like to play with him. He's fun."

Intentionally create environments in which children and adults can grow and joyfully learn together.

Design Environments That Build Community

Start by getting to know the families in your program. Learn about their expectations, perspectives, and traditions. Assess the knowledge children and families bring to your program. Invite them to share with you their valuable perspectives. A family in one of the programs we work with invited their grandfather, a famous Mexican artist, to create beautiful mosaic artwork. The children had an important opportunity to explore an authentic representation of Mexican art. The more you know the children and families, the more effectively you can engage with them.

Consider your knowledge of the neighborhood and local community. Spend time walking in the neighborhood, attending local events and community activities. Who are the local artists who can come to the program and work with the children? Explore the local natural resources to collect loose parts that children can use. Who are the local artisans who can share beautiful baskets and textiles? The more you know the community, the more you will learn about the different cultural perspectives. Attending local farmers' markets and craft fairs has provided us with wooden spoons and cooking utensils from a variety of cultures.

Explore local landmarks, and allow children the opportunity to re-create them by using the loose parts available in the environment. In our local community, we have a number of bridges. The children are familiar with them and enjoy re-creating them using a variety of blocks and loose parts.

As you learn about your community, you also get to know the wonderful people who inhabit it. They bring with them an important store of knowledge that can further support culturally sustaining environments. For example, we invited Iris Dimond, a skilled professional ceramics artist, to work with the children to explore and investigate ceramics from around the world. She also supported our efforts by sharing a number of beautiful textiles from around the world. Always reflect on your own culture, and challenge yourself to evaluate and reevaluate your own teaching practices. Begin to see diversity as the relationship that exists between you and other people you encounter. Take risks, and venture out into other communities to learn about the traditions, visual arts, and cultural values of diverse groups of people.

Cultural Sustainability in Homogeneous Classrooms

Although our communities have become more diverse, there are still many early childhood programs that remain fairly homogeneous, with children from similar cultures and backgrounds. Many early childhood programs are comprised of children who are mostly white. This may lead educators to assume that white children do not need guidance in developing a positive racial identity. Louise Derman-Sparks and Patricia Ramsey (2011) argue that, like all children, white children are actively constructing their racial identity. Therefore, educators working in homogeneous classrooms still need to think about how they can introduce diversity, communicate about diversity, and support children to positively interact with a diverse group of people. If you find yourself in this situation, here are a few suggestions.

Reflect on the possible messages you may be sending the children in your classrooms. In our eagerness to respond to children in ways that are meaningful to them, we may be creating environments that are color-blind. As professors of early childhood education and teacher preparation, we often hear our students say, "I do not have children of color, and so I do not need to teach about race and ethnicity," or "If I talk about race to children, parents get mad." Our response is to remind students of the responsibility they have to consider how biases, privilege, and power influence children's thinking and perceptions about discrimination and prejudice regardless of the demographics of the children in their programs.

Because children live and will someday work in a diverse world, they need to learn to engage positively and build equal relationships with diverse groups of people. Early childhood educators must avoid assuming that because children are not in direct contact with people of color, they are not forming ideas about people who are white or about people of color (Derman-Sparks and Ramsey 2011). Even when an early childhood program is homogeneous, we need to recognize that today all aspects of human activity, including education, are influenced by encounters with nations and people from around the world. Even though the interactions will change over time, what is certain is that we are becoming more globally interconnected.

Children notice differences and similarities at a young age, and they learn to internalize the overt and covert messages they receive from the environment. They are aware that some people in the environment are valued more highly than others. When they belong to a group that is not as highly valued, they may develop internalized oppression that makes them reject their own identity. This is how they begin to understand the concept of power and lack thereof (Derman-Sparks and Edwards 2010).

Early childhood educators must strive to validate all cultures and define diversity more broadly than just the color of a child's skin. Recognizing that white children need to have their culture validated as well is also important. Children learn about themselves and construct their identities within the context of their families and communities. Culture is beyond the color of our skin. It is comprised of rich beliefs, values, and cultural traditions. To create a positive paradigm shift, we need to go beyond embracing culture and diversity. Instead, we need to help children develop a positive identity.

Help children learn to resist and confront racial superiority. Those of us who are white need to develop our own white consciousness and recognize that we are in a powerful position to perpetuate oppressive and negative messages in our classroom, and we are also in a powerful position to make favorable changes. We need to make a commitment to create more positive realities for young children so that they can thrive in an ever-changing world. Simply stated, early childhood educators need to become allies in the work of preventing discrimination and social prejudice. Many of the strategies and ideas covered in this book can support educators working in homogeneous environments.

A strong sense of identity may help children to be more open and willing to interact with people of diverse backgrounds and spend less time putting people down. When children interact with a diverse group of children, they may be less fearful of differences and learn to find similarities. Thus, they may be encouraged to celebrate relationships and to make positive connections with people in their communities.

Our Hopes for You

We hope this book provides you many ideas for using loose parts and inspires you to design culturally sustaining environments. In our roles as professors and authors, we strive to creatively design beautiful environments where children can wonder, explore, and initiate play. We want to create spaces that allow children to take risks, develop relationships, and test their ideas. We want environments that create a sense of being for young children—places where they belong and explore who they can be in the future.

We invite you to explore the importance of beauty and aesthetics, and how these factors increase empathy and joy in early childhood programs. Take the time to meet the children and families in your classroom. Join them in learning, and invite them to bring their authentic knowledge to your environment. We hope you will embrace the dynamic nature of loose parts and bring them into the classroom with intentionality. Trust that praxis—using knowledge to inform our actions—will be created when you engage in learning together. To meet the challenges of today's classrooms, you will need to engage in ongoing critical reflection and learning. We encourage you to ask deep questions that will allow you to understand your personal identity as well as your own biases. We want this book to challenge your thinking and support you in asking more questions to guide your work with young children. It is in this reflective process that you will be able to support the cultural sustainability of early childhood environments.

Part 2
The Arts

Art

Music

Language and Literacy

The arts and humanities define who we are as a people. That is their power—to remind us of what we each have to offer, and what we all have in common. To help us understand our history and imagine our future. To give us hope in the moments of struggle and to bring us together when nothing else will.—MICHELLE OBAMA

The arts represent diverse traditions and media in every culture from around the world. Arts education spans cultural differences. Exposing children to rich experiences in visual media, language and literacy, and musical styles can validate each child's family background. Exposure also provides opportunity for children to discover and appreciate similarities and differences between their own culture and the cultures of others. When individuals actively participate in the arts, they receive inherent pleasure and recognize the importance of the arts in their lives. Additionally, as people engage with the arts, their education, aesthetic sense, and understanding of authentic culture are enhanced.

Arts education has huge benefits to children's learning. In 2009 the President's Committee on the Arts and the Humanities (2009–16) was charged with the task of reinvesting in American arts education and reinvigorating the American hallmarks of creativity and innovation. The committee's findings revealed that arts education is an effective tool in school-wide reform and a remedy to some of our nation's biggest educational challenges, such as high dropout rates and a widening achievement gap between the highest and lowest performing learners. A review of research found in *Reinvesting in Arts Education: Winning America's Future through Creative Schools* (2011) reveals the positive effect arts education has on students' academic achievement.

The benefits of art education were also addressed by John Dewey. Dewey is well known for his philosophy of education, but he also wrote a lot about art and aesthetics. In fact, his work *Art as Experience* (1934) is considered by many to have made an influential contribution to understanding the impacts of all the arts (sculpture, architecture, painting, music, drama, and literature). Dewey saw art as an experience, something that affects our lives personally, rather than just being an end product. He observed that humans have intense emotions that can be expressed through art, literature, and music and that there is an innate connection between art media and the act of expression. The implication of Dewey's work for educators is that children have the desire to tell and represent their thinking, and art, language, and music materials provide an avenue to do so.

An important component of the arts is the aesthetic need for beauty, order, and symmetry. Educators should think of the classroom environment as a home and infuse it with materials that are welcoming, visually appealing, and reflective of families and the community. Everyone's homes are filled with many captivating items of beauty, such as plants, photos, art, textures, and artifacts. Consider how each of these materials can be part of the early childhood classroom. Emphasize color, textures, natural elements, and light when displaying materials and creating play spaces. For example, line the art windowsill of your classroom with colored glass vases. The colors will be brilliant as the light from the window shines through the vases. Work on replacing plastic containers and bins with baskets from various cultures to provide a warm, natural look in the classroom. Designate display areas for art, literature, music, and found natural materials both indoors and out. Collections of pinecones, stones, and seashells are stunning and inviting in baskets, wooden bowls, or pottery. Children's sculptures look especially attractive when exhibited on textured fabric or pedestals. Frame children's art rather than just taping it to a wall. Generate curiosity by placing materials in an attractive way on tabletops using mirrors or place mats.

When choosing authentic visual art, language arts, and musical materials, consider their cultural authenticity, which is a significant attribute, according to the research of Stacey York (2016) and Wendy Lee and colleagues (2013). York highlights the importance of providing culturally relevant materials from children's home cultures and the cultures in our communities. Lee and her colleagues emphasize the relationship children have with things and how the type of materials placed in an environment cross boundaries that connect home and the early learning environment. Lee and colleagues further report on the significance of Etienne Wenger's work, which discloses that educational designs affect children's formation of identities. According to Wenger (1998), children need: "(1) places of engagement; (2) materials and experiences with which to build an image of the world and themselves; and (3) ways of having an effect on the world and making their actions matter" (271).

As educators who are responsive to diversity, we can display books about artists, authors, and musicians along with reproductions of their work that relate to children's interests. Include famous artists, authors, and musicians not only from different countries around the world but also works by men and women and in various media, such as sculpture, textiles, and mosaic. For example, Dilomprizulike of Enugu, Nigeria, is a contemporary artist working in sculpture. He calls himself the "junkman of Afrika" because of his use of discarded materials. Children may be inspired by his work to construct sculptures out of recycled loose parts. Highlight the literature of Linda Sue Park, the daughter of Korean immigrants, who has been writing since she was four years old. Among her picture books are *Mung-Mung* (2004), which describes animal sounds in different languages, and the delightful *Bee-Bim Bop!* (2005), which depicts a modern Korean American family's experience of shopping and preparing a favorite meal. Think about the addition of prominent female artists, such as Frida Kahlo (Mexican painter), Lee Krasner (American abstract expressionist painter), and Faith Ringgold (an African American artist best known for her painted story quilts).

Invite family members to share some of their culture's art, literature, and music with the children, as our friend Claudia did. Claudia is a ceramics artist and proficient potter who brought her potter's wheel to school and demonstrated its use. The children sat mesmerized as she threw the clay down in the center of the wheel and her wet hands slipped up and down the clay, changing its form with pressure. Afterward she let each child come up, placed her strong hands over theirs, and guided their hands over the wet, slick clay. She visited as a guest expert on multiple occasions, inspiring children to work with clay. After each visit, children's enjoyment could be seen as they molded their clay and then transformed their work into something else.

CHAPTER 1

Art

Imagination, investigation, self-expression, innovation, and critical thinking are all encouraged when educators support young children in developing an appreciation for art. Art experiences also teach children to take risks, be open-minded, make meaning, and be more accepting of others' differences. An adult artist flourishes in a well-provisioned studio that is visually appealing and inviting for experimenting with authentic, dynamic materials, and so do children. Use the following guidelines as you consider how to provision a studio for young children that promotes creativity.

Aesthetics: When designing an art space, fill the area with natural and artistic materials that appeal to your aesthetic senses. Bring in framed prints and artifacts of well-known artists, or a rustic, distressed vase filled with manzanita or aspen tree branches, fall leaves, or sunflowers. Aesthetics include beautiful pieces of art, striking loose parts, and the ways in which the two are combined and displayed. Windowsills lined with transparent blue glass bottles, baskets of broken pottery and birch bark, an artist's metal sculpture shown on bright kente cloth from Ghana, and a painting exhibited on an easel heighten our awareness of beauty. The type of art and how it is presented in an environment evoke emotion. Distinctive textures, varying hues, intriguing lines, and transparency all appeal to our aesthetic sense. Children are also captivated by attractive elements, such as the deep, rich earthy tones of mud cloth coupled with smooth, hard, glistening black stones and rough burlap.

Authenticity: Engage children with meaningful creative experiences. Create spaces that contain authentic artistic tools and artwork. Children need to be introduced to actual art to gain an appreciation of a work of art. Touching a genuine piece of terra-cotta is a far richer experience than touching a plastic reproduction. Exposure to real art offers opportunities for children to see similarities and differences in how a specific medium is expressed in different cultures. Think about commonalities in art media that are shared among various cultures throughout the world. Present media to children, such as paint, ceramics, mosaic, textiles, sculpture, and printing. Weaving, for example, is practiced around the world. It is seen in baskets, rugs, blankets, and clothing and is done in a variety of media. Weaving traditions are interpreted in distinctive ways and connect us to the world. To expand awareness of multicultural art, add authentic art tools for children to use in the art studio, such as clay tools, Japanese paintbrushes, and Chinese ink. Provide opportunities for children to make mosaics, designs made with small, colored materials, such as tile or glass as seen in such countries around the world as Greece, China, Italy, Mexico, and Turkey.

Equity: Equity is promoted when art-rich areas in your environment include spaces, tools, and artifacts that reflect the children's home and community cultures. All children should be welcomed and encouraged to successfully explore regardless of different abilities, interests, or learning needs. Represent family cultures through the inclusion of artwork, textiles, colors, and patterns. Consider framed ethnic fabrics, prints by well-known artists, and photos of artists in action. Display artwork on textiles, mirrors, or trays or in baskets to create inviting displays of artifacts that complement each other. It is important for all children to be exposed to art from other cultures that may not be visible in their community or may not be experienced through museum visits with their families. Physical accessibility may also be a challenge for some children. Accessible areas can be created by laying reclaimed slabs of petrified wood or stone on the floor to serve as work spaces. When a paintbrush is challenging for a child to hold, consider other painting tool options, such as sponges, loofahs, or small driftwood pieces that may be easier to grip than a standard paintbrush.

Dynamic: As you reflect on an artist's studio, consider dynamic materials to include in your own classroom that are open-ended, flexible, and conducive to creativity, curiosity, and originality. Select combinations of loose parts that allow children to both capture the essence of a work of art and manipulate the loose parts in dynamic ways. For example, if you are using a Persian brocade textile as inspiration, consider the colors, shapes, and designs reflected in the fabric when choosing accompanying materials. Include textured fabric scraps in deep violets or earthy reds, cord or ribbon in rustic golds, and materials with natural tones, such as pine needles, twigs, and leaves. These types of elements can strengthen children's critical thinking as they make meaning of what they see.

Praxis: Your role in facilitating children's creative experiences is to develop an environment with stimulating, inviting artistic materials and opportunities for children to explore. We believe that the praxis, or process of using art to create a culturally sustainable environment that encourages creativity, begins with inspiration. You can receive inspiration from works of art from all around the world by frequenting museums, art festivals, gardens, parks, bookstores, and community exhibits that feature the work of artists in a wide variety of categories, from clay and glass, to metalworking, drawing, and mixed media. Back in the classroom, use a piece of art as inspiration for children to create and design. The idea is for children to use the piece as inspiration while working with the materials rather than to merely replicate the art. Providing different media to express children's thinking allows them a chance to make meaning of their ideas—a concept inspired by the work of educators in Reggio Emilia, Italy. Remember that children's ways of using the materials may be different than yours as an educator.

Critical Reflection: Translating thoughts, perceptions, and experiences into art requires artists to use many thinking skills. Similarly, when children create a drawing or painting, they use their past and present experiences as well as imagination and emergent thinking (Fox and Schirrmacher 2015). To create art, children need to draw from their memory, observation skills, imagination, and experiences. While children are engaged in art, ask inquiry-based questions about how pieces are alike or different and what variations can be observed between pieces. Also ask open-ended questions that encourage children to think critically. For example, ask, "What might happen if you . . . ?" or "Is there another way to make your sculpture more stable?" Talk with children about their artwork, and encourage them to look closely at pieces of art from different viewpoints (front, back, top, bottom, side, close, far) and describe what they see.

From Design to Filling

Australian aboriginal fabric offers design inspiration to the delight of Martin and Elijah. The fabric design tells a story of the relationship of life, culture, and the natural world. Each story has been passed down from one generation to the next for thousands of years. A provocation is set at the table based on the fabric's abstract dot and circle designs. Teacher Miriam has offered a selection of cowry shells, glossy stones, textured paper, and burlap scraps in cream, black, taupe, and gray. Martin looks intently at the framed piece of Australian aboriginal fabric. With his fists clenched around glossy black stones, he pauses for a few seconds to study the print. He strategically places each stone inside the black picture frame in linear fashion like the dots found in the fabric. Elijah begins by placing cowry shells around the perimeter of the wooden rectangular container, eventually enclosing the whole shape. The boys' interest shifts from design work to filling the black picture frame with materials. First to go inside the frame are cowry shells. Elijah scoops up fists full of shells and releases them into the frame in rain-like fashion. Stones follow, and then buttons are placed one by one. Elijah picks up the wooden box of shells, pours, and watches the trajectory of the remaining shells as they fall into the black frame. Martin pulls the creamy fabric strips out from underneath the pile of materials. It seems as if fabric strips are not a part of their idea. Soon all the loose materials are in the frame. Elijah lifts the frame to reveal a rectangular shape of materials on the tabletop. The boys look inquisitively at the shape. Elijah places the frame back down, enclosing the materials. He shifts the frame back and forth a bit to encompass all the little pieces. Elijah picks up the frame once again. He is fascinated with the rectangular arrangement left on the table. Martin runs his hands over the materials, spreading them around. He uses a pincer grasp to pick up remaining pieces of the black fabric, holds each piece up high, and watches them fall onto the table. Both boys shift to using their palms to scoop up materials and put them back into the wooden rectangular boxes. Their exploration of designs, enclosures, and trajectory gives way to construction in the block area.

This provocation of ceramics reflects the various cultures of the families represented in the classroom and provides inspiration for the children as they work with clay.

Iris, an early childhood education professor and potter, demonstrates how to make a handle for a mug.

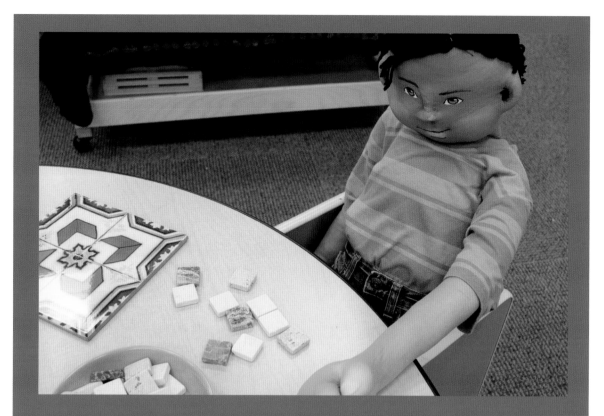

Moroccan tiles and the art of making mosaic tiles date back many centuries in Morocco. Ricky, a persona doll with Asperger's syndrome and beloved member of the classroom, joins the Moroccan setup with beautiful hand-glazed tiles in golds, creams, and grays.

Mud cloth conveys the uniqueness of Mali in a completely distinctive way. Each piece of cloth tells a story through its colors and symbols, and the way in which the symbols are arranged. The fabric serves as inspiration for Jolette and Luz to do design work.

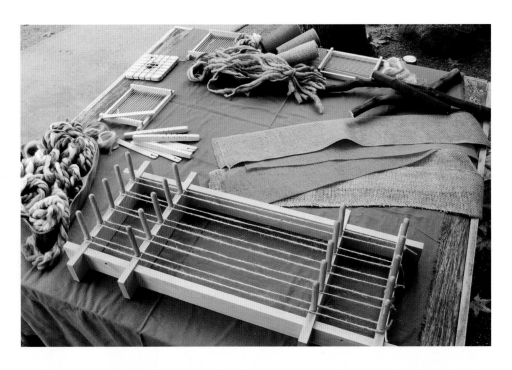

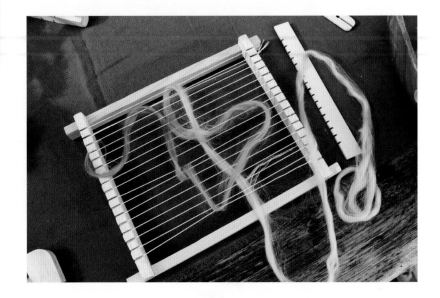

From Scottish tartans to Persian rugs and Indian saris, many types of weaving are seen in different cultures and areas. In this Northern California preschool classroom, the children's Hispanic heritage is reflected in a woven tapestry from Mexico. Thick, soft yarns and rough burlap strips complement the colors in the tapestry and offer varying textures for weaving.

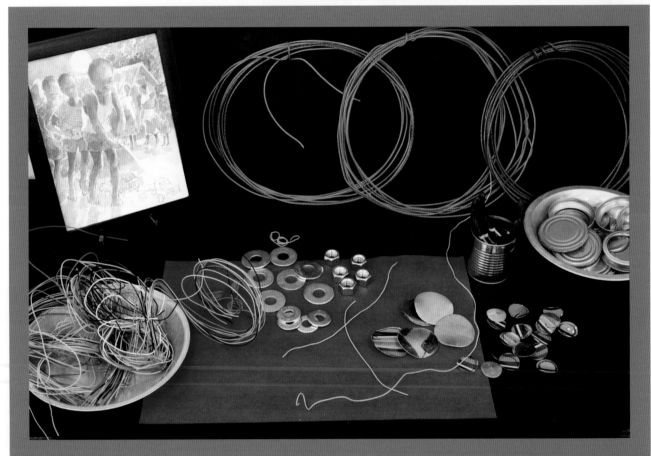

The book *Galimoto* by Karen Lynn Williams was the stimulus for an art provocation with wire. Intriguing metal loose parts of washers, nuts, and canning rings joined a variety of wire for children to create their own galimoto—a toy vehicle made of wires—or any other possibilities.

CHAPTER 2

Language
and Literacy

Literacy-rich environments are more than play spaces simply littered with print (Roskos and Neuman 1994). They are spaces filled with opportunities for children to talk and write as they investigate, negotiate, and collaborate. Children develop language and literacy skills through sustained, meaningful, and in-depth learning during play. You can support literacy play experiences by providing a wide variety of play and print materials and experiences in children's own languages to help them develop problem solving, language, and higher-level thinking. Literacy-rich environments allow children to practice their first literacy behaviors and language in ways that make sense to them (Roskos and Neuman 1994, 264). You can promote literacy by making it visible in every area of the classroom, not just isolated in reading and writing centers.

Aesthetics: Aesthetic features of literacy-rich environments include beautiful images of letters and symbols that are real representations. Find organic symbols in nature to bring into the classroom, such as a tree branch shaped like the letter *Y* or a U-shaped seedpod. Display alphabet photography of letters discovered in nature, architecture, or ordinary objects. You can also provide alphabet images of letters by artists and

graphic designers. Letters in different languages painted or drawn on real stones or wooden tree cookies are more pleasing to the eye and hand than cute caricatures made of plastic, foam, or rubber. Attractive words in metal or wood can be placed around the classroom to represent areas or activities: *art, build, explore, read.*

Authenticity: Authenticity involves provisioning a literacy-enriched play environment with loose parts that support written languages, such as recipe cards, postcards, file folders, index cards, and envelopes. When children are familiar with literacy-related items, they can rely on their prior knowledge to extend their understanding of objects through play (Neuman and Roskos 1990). Literacy artifacts reflect the diversity of cultures and help children become aware of many uses of print. Wooden alphabet blocks in, for example, English, Ukrainian, Hindi, Japanese, Spanish, or American Sign Language reveal differences among people and cultures—and blocks have the added benefit of being loose parts. Children need access to a variety of real, accessible writing tools to make their own marks (Watts and Young 2007): a variety of pencils, markers, and crayons and an assortment of materials to write on, such as stationery and journals.

On a visit to the early childhood demonstration classroom, four-year-old Rowan expressed interest in the Chinese writing she saw on a fan. In response to Rowan's interest, early childhood faculty asked Eunyoung, an art history professor at the college, if she would be willing to set up the treasured form of Korean calligraphy that she learned as a child. Eunyoung agreed and arranged her authentic calligraphy materials on top of a shelf in the environment: brushes, ink stick, signing ink, ink well/stone, stone chop, brush rest, paper, and water well. Eunyoung's provocation demonstrated to early childhood students how authentic materials and personal stories can make cultural identity visible in a significant and meaningful way.

Equity: Language is a critical aspect of culture and is recognized by the United Nations as a basic human right (UNESCO 1996). Children's language is part of their cultural identity, and individuals have a right to speak, read, and write in their home language (York 2016). You promote equity in literacy learning in early childhood environments when children have meaningful and memorable experiences that value their home languages. One way to support equity is to offer bias-free loose parts for children to use in language and literacy exploration along with books and print from family cultures.

Such opportunities can provide an avenue for children to express experiences, insights, and discoveries. For example, children can use small stones, tiles, or sticks to make alphabet characters and tell stories in any language.

Dynamic: Dynamic materials—ones that children can move, manipulate, control, and change in their dramatic play—can support children's understanding of symbolic representation (using one object or symbol to represent another). Competence in symbolic representation is necessary for learning to read and write because words and letters are symbols or representations of thoughts, objects, and verbal language. According to Jeanne Machado (2016), children with symbolic dramatic play skills have an increased ability to comprehend words and understand a variety of grammatical principles. "Small worlds," or miniature imaginative play experiences, are one way to support dramatic play opportunities. Educators can create a range of innovative and unusual small worlds, such as a dollhouse, fairy garden, moonscape, or volcanic island, using a variety of loose parts. Small-world play allows children to use symbols and language to represent objects that are not actually present and to create complex play sequences. For example, glass stones can form a river and later transform into stepping-stones. Children can express fears or relive anxious experiences, such as saving animals from a fire.

Praxis: Educators can support young children's growth in literacy skills by designing effective language and literacy environments that are enticing and engaging. Provide interesting loose parts throughout the classroom for children to develop what they need. For example, scarves can become baby slings, picnic blankets, superhero capes, or head coverings. Language and literacy skills are promoted when children have a variety of opportunities to experience meaningful and memorable things. Include purposeful print in the environment, such as recipe cards or menus in dramatic play spaces, and add items for children to imitate writing, such as restaurant order pads. Print awareness develops as children notice and understand different kinds of print on discarded postcards, business cards, or stationery with letterhead (which are all loose parts). Provide authentic learning opportunities in real-world contexts, such as cookbooks, newspapers, paper, and pens used in different cultures. According to Susan Neuman and Kathy Roskos (1997), "Participation in authentic activity, therefore, not only provides opportunity for using knowledge and strategies; it also represents critical cognitive work in literacy development" (30).

Critical Reflection: An effective literacy-rich environment encourages critical reflection and thoughtful questioning. You can engage children in inquiry through intriguing loose parts, such as sea beans, that allow children to figure something out or build new understandings. "What do you suppose these items are, and how do you think they got to be so hard and shiny?" By answering open-ended, inquiry-based questions, children have an opportunity to express their own experiences. They learn to compare how items are similar or different when they are exposed to a wide variety of multicultural artifacts that are familiar and authentic, such as eating utensils. For example, children can describe characteristics and functions of spoons from their culture. Fill the environment with written languages other than English and languages spoken by families in the classroom as a way for children to become aware of differences. Ask questions about what children are seeing and doing. For example, ask, "Could you show how your name is written in Hebrew?"

Rowan's Writing Canvas

Rowan is captivated by mark making. Her body, dirt, walls, and paper serve as her canvases. Her writing tools consist of markers, crayons, sticks, and fingers. Her early writing attempts are secret messages written on scrap paper and folded numerous times. Rowan is starting to realize that drawing and writing are different. She is recognizing letters and learning that written letters have meaning. Her scribbles are now more like print and less like art. Rowan quietly approaches the sand-writing area. Today sand is her canvas, and her finger is the writing tool. She glances at the printed words that say hello in different languages. She persists with mark making in the mint-green sand. She prepares the sand by using the palms of her hands to pull the sand into the middle of the tray, creating a mound. She pats the mound, pokes her finger into the center of the mound, and then pushes a second finger into the hole. She rubs the sand with her palms, spreading it out into a thin layer. She uses her thumb to make a long, curvy line and erases the mark. Her knowledge of linear directionality for writing English is displayed in her mark making from left to right. She makes several short, parallel lines and then a long meandering stroke that cuts through the lines. Rowan once again erases her marks and pats the sand in quick up-and-down motions. She lowers her head close to the sand tray and focuses closely on her finger. Her eyes follow her finger's movement as she makes an L shape. Underneath the L she makes a dot with tiny circular motions around and around. Her marks roughly resemble the Arabic writing above the sand tray. Rowan points to the Arabic writing and asks what it says. She is seeking the meaning of the marks, an important step in her understanding of print knowledge and writing.

As a meaningful way to support children's home languages, we placed colorful alphabet blocks in Hindi and Arabic into the demonstration classroom. The blocks give children experience with their home language and provide opportunity for discussion about print in different languages. Upon entering the environment, one college student went immediately to the letter blocks. She delighted in showing Lisa, her professor, how to spell Lisa in her native language of Hindi.

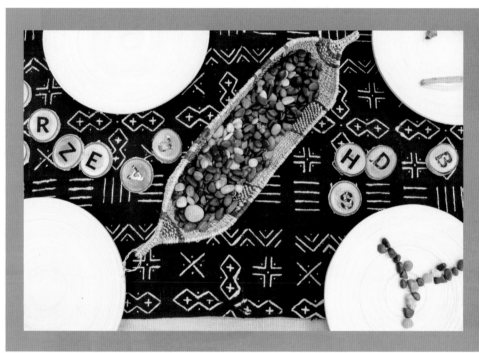

As the morning began, Yuliza stood at the literacy table. Natural elements of small stones and letters on tree cookies captivated her interest. She matched letters and then made the letter *Y* with the small stones.

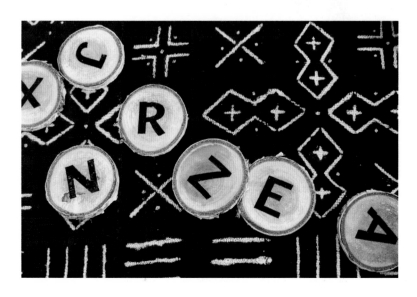

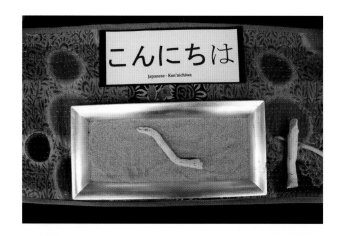

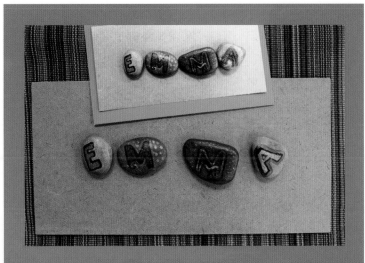

Wanting to help children gain a sense of identity, the educator in this classroom painted colorful letters on stones, took photos of rocks that spelled out each child's name, and then made name cards. The letter stones and name cards were attractively displayed for children to make representations of their names. Children not only created their own names but also made names of other children in the class.

The Worry Stone by Marianna Dengler tells the heartwarming story of how human lives are connected despite age, distance, and time. The book pays tribute to the Chumash Indians, who were the first people along the coast of California. Feathers and worry stones suggest possibilities for Leila to represent the story or create a design.

CHAPTER 3
Music

The power of music as an element of social transformation can be seen in Paraguay, South America, where young musicians play instruments that are crafted from loose parts found in a trash dump: oil cans, cutlery, wood, parts of locks, and kitchen utensils. The documentary *Landfill Harmonic* captures the poverty, illiteracy, and pollution of Cateura, a slum that is built on a landfill, and tells a story of hope, as children have learned originality, self-assurance, and community building through music's impact on their lives. The idea for sharing music with all residents of Paraguay came from Maestro Luis Szarán, a musician and conductor, who created Sonidos de la Tierra (Sounds of the Earth Orchestra). Maestro Szarian talks about music being a bridge between worlds: "Despite living under dire circumstances, if a person has initiative and is creative, even trash can become an educational tool that could change someone's life and the lives of others" (www.landfillharmonicmovie.com).

Cultural or social reform can also happen in early childhood environments through the inclusion of musical instruments from around the world that are diverse and made from unique materials. Many instruments are crafted from sustainable loose parts, such as wood, gourds, shells, metal bottle caps, and pieces of bamboo. Educators may also want to consider other upcycled materials for creating sound, such as wire coat hangers, plastic water bottles with ridges, washboards, metal coffee and trash cans, sturdy cardboard boxes and tubes, sticks, and paint stirrers.

Aesthetics: Musical instruments are inherently beautiful. Their intriguing forms, sounds, and natural materials are compelling to the eye and ear. They are gorgeous sculptures, simple and complex, made from different woods (walnut, cedar, maple, spruce, mahogany) and metals (brass, steel, bronze, aluminum), each with distinctive color, feel, and smell. An alluring way to display instruments and loose parts is to place them in decorative ethnic baskets and containers or on top of attractive cultural fabrics. Displaying instruments beautifully acknowledges the instruments' value, reflects diversity, and adds richness through the color and texture of materials.

Authenticity: Create a magnificent collection of authentic musical instruments from around the world by asking friends and family members to bring back small instruments when they travel abroad. Such was the case with Jenna, who brought back an elephant bell from Thailand. The bell, worn around an elephant's neck, is hand sculpted from wood and has clappers that strike together, announcing an elephant's movement. The children in Jenna's classroom discovered that the organic sound made by the bell is different than the sound made by the copper and brass nana bells from India, even though both bells have wooden clappers. Investigate places to buy cultural instruments in your own community, large cities, and open markets when you travel. You may find wind instruments, such as wooden or bamboo pan flutes, ceramic ocarinas, and brass pennywhistles. You might discover imported ethnic world goods in colorful stores in your own community. When selecting instruments, think about commonalities of instrument types. For example, how are different types of shakers similar? Consider a collection of percussion instruments: rhythm sticks, tabla (Indian drum), djembe (African drum), bodhran (Irish hand drum), shekere (West African gourd with shells), maracas or guiros (Latin America), caxixi (Brazilian bells), gungaroos (Indian ankle bells), and doumbeks (Middle Eastern percussion instrument).

Equity: Music is an avenue for bringing children of diverse backgrounds together, as it resonates with our hearts and souls in a way that no other medium does. Music also fosters development and learning, so children should have access to high-quality music education from a very early age. To be equitable, music needs to be an important component of every early childhood program. Culturally relevant music experiences honor children's families and introduce children to the home cultures of other children. Educators can learn about music in the family lives of children and invite families to share songs from their childhoods. When designing music spaces in the environment, be certain to play music and include instruments from different cultures.

An educator friend of ours commented about the importance of music in early childhood. "I must admit that I have strong biases about music in the classroom. When both of my adult children were in preschool, I regularly took my guitar and banjo to a YMCA in Brooklyn, New York, where my kids were enrolled. One day a mother whose roots were in Puerto Rico and whose daughter was in my son's class asked if she could join in and sing with me. We sang some Spanish and English songs that we both knew. She played the guitar and some rhythm instruments. A few weeks later, a Chinese grandfather became the third member of our unlikely trio. We taught the children (and ourselves) songs in several languages and played on authentic instruments. I think the power of multigenerational family members bringing their musical talents and instruments to the preschool classroom is a wonderful experience for both children and adults. To take my story full circle, I continued performing at my children's elementary school after we moved to the Midwest. Not too long ago, I was at a grocery store and a young woman came up to me and asked, 'Didn't you used to sing for us at Island Lake School?' I said that I did. She said, 'You were Maggie's dad, weren't you?' I told her that I still was! She went on to say how some of her fondest memories from elementary school are about singing along with her friends as I led them with my guitar. She told me that she had taught her young daughter 'The Marvelous Toy' by Tom Paxton, one of the songs I sang with the kids at the school. I believe every early childhood classroom should be filled with music."

Dynamic: Instruments are dynamic in nature. They are fascinating to children because the sounds they produce are intriguing, immediate results. Children are fascinated by sound-producing loose parts, many of which are recycled materials (washboards, roasting pans, woks, galvanized trash lids, metal colanders). Take music outdoors by constructing a sound garden where children can make rhythmic patterns. Children will discover other possibilities for making sounds by banging suspended lids, pots, pans, tin cans, pie tins, old hubcaps, and so on. Often the simplest materials and actions create the greatest pleasure. Children delight in scraping a spoon along the wooden slats of a fence or striking a pot. Hang wind chimes, gongs, and handmade bells from around the world. At Roseville Community Preschool, the teachers took giant metal pipes (loose parts), which were about three inches in diameter and up to four feet in length. They set up a pulley system to raise and lower the metal chimes into a large ceramic pot of water. Children tapped on the chimes with a rubber-tipped drumstick as the chimes dipped in and out of the water. They discovered that the pitch changed as the pipes went up and down, much to their delight and amazement.

Praxis: You can create an environment with musical materials and music listening that reveals children's musical home environments. Musical materials that you place in the environment send a message to children that these things are valuable. Begin by asking families in your program to contribute recordings of music from the children's home cultures. Educators can incorporate these recordings into music gatherings and as background music throughout the day. Investigate musical instruments related to family backgrounds. Ask the children's families to help you start a collection of authentic instruments from different cultures, and explore the musical similarities. For example, what types of rhythm sticks and drums are played? How are they alike or unalike? Display a wide assortment of instruments along with intriguing sound-making loose parts for children to experiment with sound. For example, compare gourds or seedpods with dry seeds that rattle alongside maracas for shaking. Set cardboard tubes or sections of bamboo next to flutes for blowing through, or compare tin cans and wooden boxes with drums for pounding.

Critical Reflection: Exploration with sound-producing materials helps children with critical thinking as they learn that there are differences between instruments and the sounds they make. Critical thinking transpires as children investigate sound types and basic music concepts, such as duration (sounds may be long or short), volume (sounds may be loud or soft), tempo (sounds may be fast or slow), pitch (sounds may be high or low), and timbre (sounds have distinctive characteristic qualities).

Trash Can Percussion

The children return from spring break and discover that a sound garden has been created in the play yard corner. Bright, colorful fabrics softly drape above the wooden stage. Pots, pans, and trays are secured to the white wrought iron fence with rope, while galvanized trash can lids, broiling pans, and wire racks are suspended from the pergola. Bayron and Rose are drawn to the curious selection of instruments. They experiment by banging on the objects with unusual loose parts that serve as drumsticks—intriguing spoons, strangely shaped whisks, wire-mesh strainers, whisk brooms, brushes, and metal ladles. They discover the variety of sounds that are made with different "drumsticks." *Bang, whoosh, clang, bong, whack, crash, grate, twang, swish*—each stroke of a utensil creates its own sound against the eclectic collection of drums. Sound waves vibrate throughout the yard. Their musical sounds rise to a crescendo.

The next day, Bayron's great passion for exploring different banging sounds continues, but his interest switches to the inverted trash cans. He starts his rhythm with two drum mallets made with tennis balls on the ends of wooden dowels. He rhythmically pounds the inverted rubber trash can with the tennis balls. His drum mallets are held in matched grip, with palms facing down and elbows relaxed at his side, as if he were a drummer in a rock band. Low, deep tones reverberate. He experiments with where he gets the most bounce when he thumps the mallets. Next, Bayron adjusts to a tighter grip and taps the wooden dowels against the trash can's rimmed edge, making a higher, tight pitch. He changes drums from the rubber trash can to the galvanized one and makes a tin sound with sharper, faster beats. He engages in different drumming techniques as he plays beats in steady strokes, creating a constant pulse, and then in odd patterns that make totally unique sounds.

While observing Bayron's drumming interest, teacher Lisa recalls a performance she attended of the Afro-Cuban Funk Band at Folsom Lake College. She had been captivated by the musicians' "Frankensteinesque" sound, which is a mix of "Afro-Bet, West African High Life, Latin Jazz and Salsa, BeBop, Ska, and Reggae with a heavy dose of Funk." She decides to bring in recordings of their music along with other types of Latin drumming influences from Africa and Cuba to foster Bayron's drumming passion and expose the children to distinctive cultural music.

An elephant bell from Thailand adds interest to a sound garden of bells.

After observing a group of children fascinated with drumming, the educators set up an intriguing variety of drum surfaces to tap on.

Oh, the joy of shaking maracas and experiencing the immediate effect of a delightful noise! Children are intrinsically motivated to produce sound with shakers that are made from upcycled or natural loose parts.

Part 3
Inquiry

Engineering

Science and Math

Sensory Exploration

The questions we ask are often more important than the answers we search for. Every question leads to particular lines of inquiry.—KEN ROBINSON

Children are active and confident learners who develop inquiry dispositions such as curiosity, resourcefulness, purposefulness, collaboration, persistence, and creativity when they explore meaningful, inquiry-rich environments. An inquiry-rich environment that is culturally relevant opens children's minds and provokes wonder, curiosity, and intellectual engagement (Curtis and Carter 2003). It is in an active learning environment where children have opportunities to investigate and engage with a variety of flexible and open-ended loose parts. These interactions help children learn to make meaning of their experiences, expand their learning, and reexamine their ideas. According to Australia's Early Years Learning Framework (2009), "Children are more likely to be confident and involved learners when their family and community experiences and understandings are recognized and included in the early childhood setting. This assists them to make connections and to make sense of new experiences" (32). Environments need to contain materials that recognize the cultures of families enrolled in the program and foster investigation and inquisitiveness. We can provoke children's exploration through engaging and fascinating loose parts, such as cove molding, gutters, wooden planks, tubes, and drainpipes, along with a variety of different items that roll (balls, pinecones, wooden spools, logs, tin cans, and wheels). Materials need to be accessible and readily available for children so they can reach them independently and instantly. When children can access materials immediately, they can pursue their ideas and continue their investigations without interruption.

Through active, hands-on experiences, children develop scientific skills, becoming keen observers, investigators, problem solvers, communicators, and critical thinkers. Observation skills involve the use of all our senses to collect information about objects and events.

· ·

Sammy notices the long, corrugated black pipe that has been cut lengthwise to resemble a gutter and attached to the white picket fence in serpentine fashion. He approaches the gutter pipe with balls in hands and wonders about where to drop the ball in the pipe's trench. He places a white plastic ball at the top of the gutter pipe, releases it, and pauses for a second to watch the ball roll. The ball quickly speeds down the gutter pipe and at the halfway mark bounces out of the gutter onto the ground. He tries placing a second ball at the top of the gutter pipe, which results in the ball bouncing out of the pipe in the same location as the first ball.

Sammy has encountered a problem. He investigates the pipe and gathers evidence about the balls' trajectories by looking down the pipe's center to see

where the ball rolled off and runs his hand along the gutter. He wonders why the balls do not roll along the entire length of pipe. His solution to the problem is to change the starting position of the ball. He places the ball lower on the gutter pipe rather than at the very top. This time the ball rolls the remaining distance of the gutter pipe and falls off at the end. He communicates his finding to John, who has been watching close by.

Sammy points, "See, it comes off here, so I start it here."

His experimentation continues by trying smaller wooden balls. Critical thinking follows as he notices that the wooden balls roll at a faster rate than the white plastic balls and that they also stay in the gutter. His evaluation will result in a theory of ball type, incline, and trajectory speed.

Chalufour and Worth state, "Science for young children is about investigating real things, developing new ideas and theories, and sharing them with others. The richer and more varied the environment is, the richer and more varied the experiences the children will have" (2004, 8). Environments support science and inquiry when provisioned with upcycled loose parts for children to invent, design, build, construct, explore, and solve problems. Much of our learning comes from doing. Children need real materials to investigate engineering, science, math, and sensory concepts. As you consider materials for your inquiry environment, consider items that will provoke children to explore, formulate ideas, and apply previous learning to new situations.

CHAPTER 4
Engineering

Engineering environments need to be filled with materials that inspire an architect, contractor, and engineer. Ingrid Chalufour and Karen Worth (2004) say that such an environment should convey the excitement, challenge, and wonder of building with different types of materials. There needs to be opportunity to tinker and investigate. Researchers Gold, Elicker, Choi, Anderson, and Brophy (2015) identified the following common engineering play behaviors in young children:

- communicating goals
- designing and constructing
- solving problems
- creating/innovating ideas
- testing/evaluating
- explaining how things are built/work
- following patterns and prototypes
- thinking logically and mathematically
- using technical vocabulary

To foster these play behaviors, design indoor and outdoor engineering environments with aesthetic, authentic, and dynamic materials that compel builders and engineers and naturally support praxis, critical reflection, and equity. How do our six guiding words help us design engineering environments?

Aesthetics: Appealing wooden materials include blocks, planks, and tree blocks in varying characters, colors, smells, and textures. Consider the beauty of walnut's dark chocolate brown or oak's swirling, water-like pattern. Some woods have distinctive smells, including the woody, fishy smell of driftwood. Display intriguing shapes and uniform sizes of plastic pipe in ways that contribute to their attractiveness. Placing materials in wooden containers wrapped in rope or in ethnic baskets highlights their beauty. Encourage children to build and reflect on the importance of community by mounting photographs of local landmarks (such as bridges and buildings) on the walls.

Authenticity: Susan Neuman and Kathy Roskos (1990) recommend that materials in an early childhood environment be authentic (found in an adult setting) and functional (practical and useful). Gather common building materials from community sources and family members to serve as loose parts. You can also purchase real building materials (lumber, tile, molding, gutters), plumbing supplies (pipes and fittings), and electrical materials (wire and cable spools) at local hardware stores, general stores selling salvaged goods, re-stores, and upcycle centers. Consider materials that differ in material, shape, texture, size, and weight. Provide large quantities of pieces that are uniform in shape and size. For example, cut 4 × 4 wood posts into lengths of 4-, 8-, and 12-inch pieces. For constructing in your environment, provide wooden blocks, cubes, cylinders, cones, and arcs. For engineering, include ramps/planks, cove molding, pipes/tubes, gutters, and sawhorses. Add loose parts that roll: balls, cable spools of wood or sturdy cardboard, rings, and wheels. Irregular materials, such as tree branches cut into sections or scraps from a lumberyard, also make interesting building materials and present different construction challenges.

Equity: Engineering areas in your environment can promote equity when engineering materials are diverse and accessible to all children. Engineering problems inherently allow for multiple solutions rather than a single right answer, so children have the opportunity to be successful using loose parts in varying ways to solve problems. In designing engineering spaces with equity, think about design modifications you may need to make so that all children, including those with disabilities, can engage with engineering loose parts. This may involve modifying space or placement of materials for easy access.

Dynamic: Loose parts may be used in endless ways for designing, constructing, solving problems, innovating, and testing ideas. Provide a rich and diverse supply of building materials that are loose parts from your community for children to build towers, bridges, enclosures, and structures. Children can also experiment with the physics of force, acceleration, gravity, trajectory, velocity, rotation, and direction. In Anji, China, for example, engineering-specific loose parts consist of bamboo poles and ladders, tires, wooden planks, blocks in various sizes, barrels, and sawhorses (www.anjiplay.com). In addition to materials listed in the section on authenticity above, include the following open-ended materials for building: stones, tree stumps, tree cookies, logs, crates, cardboard boxes, empty cans, and thread spools. Add materials for connecting: string, rope, twine, yarn, and chain. Avoid providing tape and glue for engineering spaces, because once loose parts are attached, they are no longer loose and reusable. Attaching materials without the use of adhesive is a challenge that requires problem solving (How can I get these materials to stay together without tape or glue?).

Praxis: Engineering experiences are based on real-world problems. Give children hands-on experiences now to help their understanding of abstract math and science concepts that will be introduced in the future; that is, open-ended exploration with building and engineering materials provide a concrete foundation for advanced thinking. Through engaging in relevant experiences with loose parts, children can see how the math and science of engineering relate to real-life circumstances. To design engineering-rich environments that support praxis, provide engineering loose parts, challenges, and vocabulary. Inform and transform your practice by learning the language of engineering to engage children in the inquiry process and to foster critical thinking. Make physics terms, such as *balance*, *energy*, *impact*, *resistance*, *static*, and *projectile*, part of your conversations with children. Encourage children to observe, predict, test, reflect, and conclude to solve problems.

Critical Reflection: An environment that is rich in engineering possibilities can foster critical reflection. Through construction experiences, children acquire science inquiry skills, including wondering, questioning, exploring, investigating, discussing, reflecting, and formulating ideas and theories (Chalufour and Worth 2004). Engineers are naturally curious and inquisitive, just like children. They want to know how and why things work. Encourage children to think like engineers by helping them identify and articulate problems they encounter. For example, say, "I see that you spread the blocks farther apart at the base. What was your reason for doing so? What happened when you did that?" Challenge their thinking: "You told me that the ramp needed to be lowered for the ball to roll to the carpet, but I see that you raised it instead. What were you thinking when you changed ideas?" Guide children to brainstorm possible solutions and test their theories to deepen reasoning: "What else might you do to make your structure more stable? Try it out, and see what happens."

Tubes and Towers

During group gathering, the children are fascinated by a photograph of the Eiffel Tower in a book. A spark ignites, excited discussion occurs, and enthusiastic engineers begin to construct towers. A canvas picture of the Eiffel Tower is hung on the wall of the construction area. Later, photos of the Eiffel Tower and other tall towers from around the world are put in acrylic frames and placed on top of the block shelves as inspiration. The teachers notice children moving the photos to the floor and studying them intently as they build towers. Different building materials are added alongside wooden blocks to foster the children's interest in tower building. Materials include a community donation of large cardboard tubes (cores from butcher paper rolls) and cardboard yarn cone winders, upcycled from a textile company. The teachers challenge the children by asking which materials will build the tallest tower. Children discover that the type of building material and construction influences the stability of a tall tower.

Isa takes cardboard tubes and builds two parallel towers; each tower stacked three tubes high. He grasps a tube in each hand and simultaneously places one more tube on each tower. Bayron stands off to Isa's side and aids by holding a tube in each of his hands. Kolton enters the construction zone and points to the Eiffel Tower photo. He gives instruction on how to build the tower. His plan is to place a cone on top. Keliah joins the discussion, and an argument transpires. Keliah points to the Eiffel Tower photo and says that it needs to be built tall. Isa agrees with her assessment and affirms that the tubes will make it taller. Kolton insists that a cone is needed for the top, as the Eiffel Tower has a point. Bayron and Vivian watch as Isa adds another tube, making each tower six tubes high. The towers are now past each child's shoulders in height. Isa grasps two tubes that are longer and thinner than the previous ones. He hands one to Kolton. Isa and Kolton each hold their tubes up high to add a seventh level. Kolton places his tube on top. As he lets it go, it drops and falls through the tower of tubes, causing the tubes to fall over. Isa watches but decides not to add the seventh tube to his tower. He places the narrower tube back on the shelf.

An investigation about bridges provides opportunity to compare types of bridges from our community and world. Children's learning and excitement are enhanced as they share their own experiences of traveling across bridges, and build with a wide variety of interesting construction materials. They discover that certain designs make bridges stronger and more stable.

Beam Bridge

Equity is promoted when girls have an opportunity to build. Maddox and Ashlyn have strong ideas about how to build a castle. An argument occurs about the design process, and neither girl is fond of the other's idea. After expressing their views, they eventually negotiate a solution that works for both of them.

Bayron and Duane watch the balls race down the inclined plank after reinforcing the ramp's sides for stability. Their plan included a barricade at the end to stop the balls from rolling across the construction area.

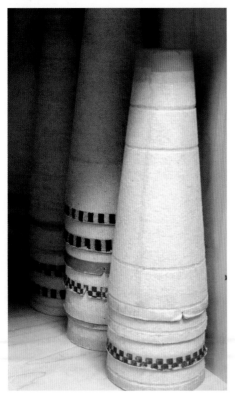

Sacramento landmarks printed on canvases provide construction inspiration and connection to the local community.

CHAPTER 5
Science and Math

Children learn science through hands-on experiences in which they construct their own understanding about what things are, how things work, and how things are connected to each other (Martin 2001). This means that children can learn to investigate problems: How can I get the water to go from here to there? or, How can I make the water move a different way? Mathematical learning emerges in the same way as science concepts, by engaging in meaningful play experiences with real objects (Seo 2003). Math learning includes an understanding of number and operations, algebra, geometry, measurement, and data analysis and probability. Science and math are interrelated, as both content areas rely on an inquiry-based approach. Children acquire science and math concepts as they play indoors and outdoors with water, sand, dirt, construction materials, and manipulatives, as well as during art, literacy, dramatic play, and cooking experiences. Educators can contribute to children's natural curiosity and inquisitiveness by creating culturally sustainable environments with multitudes of rich science and math materials. How do our six guiding words support environments rich in science and math?

Aesthetics: Stepping-stones can add beauty to a playscape and support scientific understanding. Logs of varying wood types, sizes, and interesting design features provide attractiveness and lend themselves to innovative explorations as children move them around or balance on them. River rocks, stones, and pebbles exhibit an extraordinary splendor when wet. Water basins and troughs carved from natural granite or wood for water play are pieces of art. Include visually appealing math materials for children to classify, count, pattern, and seriate—seashells, pinecones, acorns, sea glass, tree cookies, and tiles. A thoughtful array of tiles and stones made of different materials (aluminum, ceramic, glass, marble, and metal), color families (beige, black, blue, gray, metallic, purple), and various shapes, sizes, styles, textures, and designs offer their own visual magnificence when displayed artistically. Abalone shells or implements made out of wood for use as digging tools provide unmatched beauty compared to a plastic shovel.

Authenticity: Real objects allow children to compare similarities and differences. For example, children can see contrast as they use different types of ladders (bamboo, rope, wooden), planks, nautical rope, and sawhorses. Authentic water tools include real tools that could be used in actual water situations, for adults and children alike: containers of various sizes and shapes; galvanized water troughs, tubs, and buckets;

funnels; test tubes and beakers; basters; pipettes; colanders; measuring cups; hand mixer; and ladles. Measurement tools from different cultures are used for measurement by adults and children and are made from varying materials. Some examples are measuring cups (solid and liquid), measuring spoons, scales (digital, market, food, balance), rulers, calculators, hourglasses, and abaci. Offer children explorations with measuring instruments and real materials in sand and water and provide intriguing things to measure. Provide opportunities for children to weigh, measure, and compare by adding loose parts such as buttons, thread spools, nuts, bolts, washers, and keys.

Equity: The classroom reflects the values we have identified as important to us. Our personal experiences and social influences, such as gender, culture, and family background, can affect our attitudes toward math, science, and technology. What we believe about math, science, and technology can result in inequities (Prairie 2005). For example, we may believe that girls are not well suited for careers in engineering and discourage girls from engineering play. A science-rich environment planned for investigation invites all children across gender, culture, ability, economic status, and geographic areas to freely explore. A teacher's disposition toward thoughtfulness, reflection, and cultural competence can impact children's understanding of equity. Shaun Murphy (2012) describes how the children in his class demonstrated an understanding of inequality and represented it through mathematics. After reading *The Rabbits* by John Marsden (2003), Murphy asked the children to use Cuisenaire rods to explore the power issues they had read about in the book. *The Rabbits* is a story about the colonization of Australia in which European colonists are portrayed as rabbits, and Aborigines are portrayed as kangaroos. First-grader Kerry explained the relationship between power and amount: she said that there were fewer rabbits, but they had more power because their thirteen rods were worth more than the kangaroos' twenty-five rods (Murphy 2012, 19).

Dynamic: Free play with water can build the foundation for understanding physic concepts of flow and motion, chemistry concepts of solutions and cohesion, and mathematics concepts of measurement, equivalence, and volume (Gross 2012, 3). To support development of these concepts, include the following dynamic materials in the environment: gutters, pipe (black corrugated, rain gutter, bamboo, gutters and downpipes, water), pipe connectors (straight and with varying degrees of bends to create a change of direction), water pumps, and watering cans. Many children are fascinated by the task of transporting materials from one place to another. Support children's interests by providing dynamic tools for transporting: wheelbarrows, wagons, farm canisters, baskets, gourds, and buckets along with materials to transport, such as pieces of chain, sand, water, wooden rings, and pinecones.

Praxis: Children's exploratory play supports development of basic science skills, such as making predictions, gathering evidence, and drawing conclusions, and math skills, such as measurement and estimation. Early childhood educators need to understand the nature of scientific inquiry, its central role in science, and how to use the skills and processes of scientific inquiry (Martin 2001, 6). Expand your personal expertise by investigating an area of science or math for your own inquiry. Experiment with materials so you can acquire firsthand understanding about materials and scientific concepts. According to Ingrid Chalufour and Karen Worth, "In order to be responsive to children's explorations, you need to recognize and experience the science phenomena children are experiencing" (2004, 7). Your role is to design outdoor and indoor spaces for children to explore physical and earth sciences. This can be done by including multiple spaces for water play (tabletops and sand), smooth-surfaced areas for construction, and sand areas for digging.

Critical Reflection: As you develop science and math spaces, consider how children's engagement with science and math materials can encourage critical reflection. Children acquire information from manipulating items, trial and error, input from other children and adults, watching, and listening. Inquiry processes used by children include exploring, identifying, classifying, comparing and contrasting, hypothesizing, and generalizing (Feeney, Christensen, and Moravcik 2016). Help children advance and deepen their thinking as they use these inquiry processes to solve problems. Observe children's actions and listen to their theories to capture the process of inquiry in the making. Question their thinking, and determine materials to place in the environment that can extend their exploration. Mia and Sam play together at a long trough containing sand and lightly running water. The children investigate how the water pools or flows when the river's pathway is blocked, released, or directed. The teacher engages the children in the scientific process of exploring, comparing and contrasting, and hypothesizing as the children experiment with the water's movement. The teacher asks, "Where do you think it's going to break? How can you get the water to go over the edge like a waterfall?"

Zip Line Challenge

Teacher Jenna sets the stage for scientific inquiry with rich, varied objects. In a large, open sand area, she arranges an abundance of large loose parts: pieces of plywood, palm tree trunks, wire cables, chunks of wood that resemble blocks, wood planks, two-by-fours, and mini sawhorses. This large construction provocation offers infinite investigation possibilities. Children use problem solving to make an obstacle course by connecting materials in different ways. During the construction process, children build science concepts about gravity, tension, stability, and balance. Teacher Michael challenges the children to make the obstacle course longer so they can go from the zip line to the end of the play yard without touching the ground. Children build a balance beam structure with wooden planks and sawhorses. They lean additional planks at an angle on either side of the beam to serve as ramps for getting on and off. Six large plastic spools are stacked in two piles next to the ramps. Addy approaches the ramps and stands in front of one of them looking at it with a furrowed brow. Noah kicks over one pile of spools. "Don't do that! This is an obstacle course!" Addy exclaims. Slowly Addy takes small steps onto the ramp made by the first wooden plank. She places both hands on either side of the plank. As she grasps the sides, she scoots her feet up the ramp and then climbs off at the top. She climbs up the ramp a second time, but this time she keeps her arms spread out. Addy repeats this climbing strategy several times. Then Addy runs up one ramp, stops at the top, steps over to the next ramp, and runs down. "Look how fast I can run up and down," Addy yells to Easton. After watching Addy repeat the cycle, he follows Addy up the ramp and back down. Upon his arrival at the center, Walker races outdoors to discover that the intriguing materials have been made into an obstacle course by the previous class. He calls the area a video game and invites Easton to play the video game with him. Walker first shows Easton which direction to go to complete the level. Every day children from different classes add to and extend the obstacle course. Throughout the weeks, each class modifies the area and builds on previous work. This is a true sign that the children are applying physical science concepts, such as varying actions to affect outcomes, as they experiment with inclined planes.

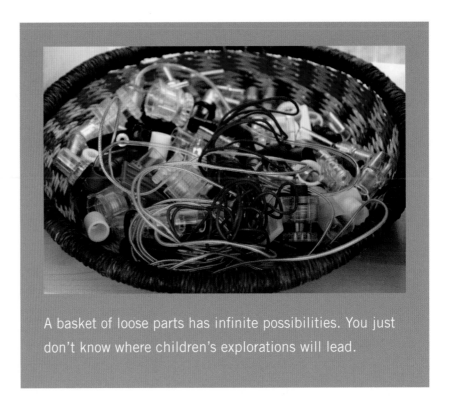

A basket of loose parts has infinite possibilities. You just don't know where children's explorations will lead.

Large patterned buttons offer potential for classifying, patterning, counting, and ordering.

Intriguing materials beckon children's sense of curiosity and adventure. How will the children move the nautical docking rope up the plank to the ship's deck?

Michael listens as the water spray from the hose nozzle clashes with the metal and watches in fascination as the water spray forcefully smacks the metal wok and then whirls around the large metal bowl.

CHAPTER 6

Sensory Exploration

Sensory exploration includes play with materials that stimulate a child's senses: sight, touch, hearing, smell, and taste. Play with natural elements, such as water, sand, and clay, fosters critical thinking by providing children opportunities to use their senses in novel and meaningful ways. Most children are drawn to the soothing and enjoyable sensation of water and the feeling of warm and grainy sand slipping between their fingers. And when the two textures meet, new possibilities emerge. The sheer delight of these materials can invite children to explore and invent new ways to use them. Children need intentional materials, spaces, and opportunities to actively use their senses as they investigate the world. To foster sensory exploration, create indoor and outdoor environments for children with aesthetic, authentic, and dynamic materials that awaken children's senses and inherently support praxis, critical reflection, and equity.

Aesthetics: When designing sensory areas in your environment, include natural objects and elements, such as sand, clay, and water, that entice children's visual, olfactory, and tactile senses. Display collections of natural loose parts, such as pinecones, rocks, feathers, and seashells, in woven baskets. Sands come in multiple varieties from diverse deserts and mountains. Each type is a sensory delight of color: silky orange-red desert sand, earthy light Mojave beige, and sparkly white stardust. Some sands change hues when wet or under different light; some have smooth grains, others rough textures. Clay ranges in color from sandy white and light cream, to gray, tan, and rich reds and browns. The texture of clay changes to slippery with the addition of water, and it becomes more malleable as you work with it. Spices presented in small glass or metal containers provide splendid visual appeal in assorted shades of greens, yellows, and browns. Wonderful aromas fill the air as you grind blends of herbs and spices: sprigs of rosemary, cloves, cinnamon sticks, and seeds (anise, cardamom, celery, coriander, cumin, fennel, and mustard).

Authenticity: Authentic tools are tools used by adults and made to accomplish tasks effectively and efficiently. For example, it takes less effort to dig compacted dirt or sand with a metal scoop than a plastic one. When children use authentic tools in sensory spaces, they learn about the functionality of tools and gain competence in manipulating them. For sensory play with water and sand, include authentic tools made from wood and metal for scooping, pouring, and sifting. Funnels, sifters, scoops, colanders, containers, sieves, and kitchen tools are examples. Provide ladles, sieves, and pitchers from countries around the world that vary in design and differ in size, shape, and the material of which they are made. For clay, provide real potter's tools for shaping, flattening, smoothing, and trimming clay—metal or ceramic scrapers, wooden modeling tools, sponges, rollers, and ribs. Also, include authentic sculpting tools for creating impressions in clay, such as sculpting thumbs, ridged seashells, and textured rollers. Exploration with sand, water, and clay is enhanced with the addition of authentic natural loose parts that are native to your community: coconut shells, rocks, pebbles, wood pieces, and shells.

Equity: Sensory-rich areas in your environment can promote equity by using sustainable materials, creating accessibility, and providing alternative tactile options. Sand, rocks, driftwood, gravel, crushed shells, and clay suggest many sensory exploration possibilities and are sustainable. Create access for children to engage in sensory explorations by placing trays or tubs of materials on a table or floor. These options allow children to sit beside the tub or lie on their tummy to access materials with their hands or feet. Containers and utensils of different shapes and sizes accommodate various grasps so children may successfully use tools. Providing alternative tactile options supports multiple differences and equity. For children who have a gluten allergy, offer clay that is gluten-free instead of playdough. For children with breathing challenges, present natural sands that are clean and dust- and dye-free. For children who may have an aversion to touching certain tactile materials, provide tools such as cooking utensils. Offering children food products, such as flour, rice, or beans, for sensory play needs careful consideration because it will affect children from multiple backgrounds and with food sensitivities. While food-related materials may provide intriguing sensory explorations, many educators, including we authors, find it hard to justify playing with food while millions of children in the world live in poverty and hunger. We believe that playing with food is wasteful and disrespectful when food is expensive and hard to come by for many families around the world, including in our own country. You will need to consider the pros and cons of using food for play and make your own decision.

Dynamic: Tools for rich sensory exploration are naturally dynamic, as they produce actions of pouring, digging, sifting, transporting, transforming, and rotating. When choosing tools for sensory play, consider tools for pouring: pitchers, scoops, ladles, coconut shells, funnels, cans, gourds, and containers. Digging and sifting tools include spades, shovels, scoops, trowels, sifters, colanders, and sieves. Transporting tools on the playground include pails, buckets, pots, basters, gourds, and canisters. Transforming tools such as scrapers, rakes, and trowels are good for shaping, flattening, and dragging sand. Small sand rakes, trowels, scrapers, and rubber-tipped brushes are perfect for making designs in sand on a light table or in a sand tray. Rotating tools include eggbeaters, wire whips, waterwheels, lazy Susans, utensil caddies, and sifters. The children transform clay through poking, patting, squeezing, rolling, scraping, pulling, and pushing. Kiley pokes deep holes into clay, while Erin molds a slab into a long tube.

Praxis: The practical application of effective design is to create environments filled with enticing colors and textures that stimulate children's senses. This can be done by offering natural sensory materials, such as sand, gravel, and water, that excite children's senses and inquisitive nature. Design intriguing outdoor sand areas with adequate space and drainage and access to both sun and shade. Consider framing the space with natural elements, such as logs, boulders, or river rock. Add natural loose parts and tools that are durable, authentic, and appealing. Include spaces for water exploration, and provision them with water sources and tools to transport, transform, displace, and measure water. Provide water sources, such as water in large tubs and buckets, a hose with a low-flow or conservation hose nozzle, and five-gallon water containers with spigots for children to access on their own. While water has huge play potential, it is a valuable resource that is scarce in many parts of the world. It is important to create ways to conserve water and find innovative ways to capture, divert, and store rainwater for later use.

Critical Reflection: Early childhood educators can foster children's problem-solving and reasoning skills as children engage with sensory-rich materials. Jessica Whittaker (2014) says teachers exhibit problem-solving behaviors when they "help children form questions about what they observe and make predictions, share their own thinking and problem-solving processes aloud with children, model and conduct experiments to test predictions, and facilitate discussion about the results of children's experiments" (83). As children pursue open-ended sensory explorations, you will have many opportunities to promote critical reflection by using key phrases like the following:

- What do you think caused it to change?
- What do you think would happen if you _____?
- What did you see happening?
- How did you make that work?
- What is a new way to make that work? Why did you choose _____ over _____?
- How are they the same? Different?

Your actions will help children notice cause-and-effect relationships, form and test theories, and consider different solutions to problems.

From Drought to Downpour

For the past several years, basically the entire lifetime of current preschoolers, California has been in a drought. With the extreme water shortage, opportunities for water play have been limited. Instead, during outdoor play, children have been exploring the texture of dry sand as it cascades off shovels and fills buckets. Time is spent smoothing, piling, sifting, and patting the dry substance. Isa and

Bayron have been carving roads that lead to Folsom Lake. Conversations take place about family trips to Folsom Lake and how there is no water for playing in. The boys build a representation of the dry lake bed and stack heavy river rocks along the lake's perimeter. Keliah sits in the dry bed and comments on the lake bed's soft feel as she makes arcs in the fine sand with large sweeping motions. The next month arrives, and everything changes. Heavy rains come and saturate the sand. The damp sand is moldable and can be lightly pressed into a variety of different shapes. Children are completely absorbed with the transformation of sand and water into wonderful mud. Renewed enthusiasm for building Folsom Lake emerges. Pooled water is

carried by children in containers and poured into the lake bed. As the water level in the lake rises, conversations shift to storms, flooding creeks and rivers, and the breaking spillway at Lake Oroville, which is eighty miles north of the preschool. Children express concern about the Folsom Lake dam breaking as well and decide to reinforce their dam. Extra river rocks are added, and wet, gritty sand is molded and patted to make high sides around the lake. Workers gather each time there is a break in the lake, and they work with urgency to "fix it strong and safe."

Marlysa is fascinated with repetitively filling and emptying a multitude of different containers with water.

Mortars and pestles are available from a wide variety of cultures, from Vietnam to central and West Africa, Mexico, Egypt, and Italy. They can be found in various sizes and be made of granite, marble, porcelain, wood, glass, and metal. Here children experience wonderful aromas as they grind dried basil, parsley, oregano, and thyme for marinara sauce.

Inviting spaces to investigate natural clay allow children opportunity to express their creativity and ideas, process emotions, and research questions. Children need daily access to clay and time to learn how to manipulate it and use the tools.

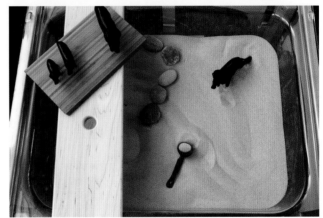

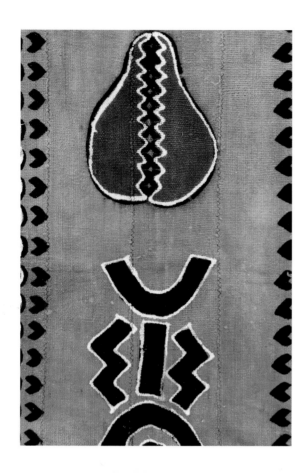

Part 4
Daily Living

Cooking Spaces

Imaginative Play

Nurturing, Empathy, and Caring

We all live with the objective

of being happy: our lives are all

different and yet the same.

—ANNE FRANK

Play is one of the most important parts of childhood. It is through play that children gain information about the world and increase their cultural awareness. When children play, they engage in complex sequences of symbolic representation and figure out how social rules work. Children also learn to negotiate and understand each other. An important aspect of play is pretend play, which is characterized by children's exploration and interpretation of the world in terms of symbols and images, fantasy, make-believe, expression of emotions, and their capacity to understand different situations in an imaginary context (Russ 2004). Play crosses cultural boundaries and allows children to learn to respect and be responsive to children who are different from them. Early childhood educators can take advantage of play to create environments where children can learn to play with other children, listen to different perspectives, and negotiate to share their ideas.

Psychologist Lev Vygotsky (1978) argued that make-believe play is important to help children understand societal rules, which often are imposed on them. To support this concept, the dramatic play area needs to be rich with cultural tools that characterize the children in the classroom, including common household-living props (mirrors, family photos, dishes, cooking utensils, lunch boxes, keys, phones, clocks). Make certain there are materials for manipulating, sorting, filling, and emptying. These can include boxes, cartons, bags, jars, measuring cups, pots and pans, stones, edible chestnuts, poker chips, bottle caps, and pom-poms. When the area offers a variety of cultural tools and artifacts that children can manipulate in different ways, they begin to make sense of their daily lives.

This was clearly seen in an interaction between a small group of children as they played "house." Jillian and Charlotte reenacted cooking and cleaning in the dramatic play area. Davon came over and said, "Can I play?" Simultaneously both girls said, "No." A teacher standing nearby came over and asked the girls, "Is there a role Davon can play? He really wants to be with both of you." Jillian said, "Okay." Charlotte went over to the shelves and found what looked like a briefcase and handed it to Davon. She said, "Here, you are the dad, so go off to work." Charlotte was developing a recognition of male and female roles. This was an opportunity for an educator to talk about how both males and females can go to work, or cook, or clean their house.

Play is the core for learning and self-actualization. According to psychologist Abraham Maslow (1999), people who have achieved self-actualization are autonomous and independent. Their interrelationships with family and community are healthy. It is evident that self-actualized individuals accept themselves. They have a strong sense of reality, and their personal abilities are evident. They have the ability to adapt and rise above their environments by being problem-centered rather than self-centered. They are empathic and capable of caring for others and their own well-being. Self-actualized people are creative and susceptible to "mountaintop experiences," such as joyful feelings of excitement, insight, and happiness. Meeting children's developmental needs, supporting their strengths, and creating a sense of belonging and inclusion are part of what Maslow defines as a step toward self-actualization.

The educator's role is to promote and support children's play and meaningful social interactions and to help them go beyond superficial exploration of culture. Educators can build children's understanding of the world through observing the variety of ways the children communicate who they are, how they interact with others, and what they think and how they feel.

Because play is learned within the context of culture, it is important to understand that children's play may vary from culture to culture. In 2009 Dorothy Singer and her colleagues pursued a cross-cultural comparative study on children's play. They interviewed mothers from sixteen nations in different continents. Controlling for socioeconomic status across the different countries, they found that children in more industrialized and urban cities engaged more in pretend play compared to children living in more rural and suburban areas. The rural and suburban children generally engaged in more creative activities, such as painting, drawing, and toy play. This information is important because to better support children's play, it is crucial to understand the cultural background of children in the classroom. For example, children living in a rural environment may spend time playing about farming or taking care of animals, while children living in a more urban environment may pretend to drive a car or work in a store. Children tend to re-create their daily experiences as they engage in imaginative play. By understanding the children's cultures, educators can provision the environment with loose parts and materials that better support children and engage them in collaborative play.

Loose parts offer many possibilities to enhance play that is representative and responsive to children's culture. Design dramatic play spaces that are infused with tools and loose parts from different cultures. Offer children the opportunity to explore what it is like to live in another culture alongside representations of their home culture in the environment. For example, familiar but new cultural materials might include baby carriers. Add baby dolls that look like the children in the program, ethnic fabrics, and baby carriers from around the world, such as *rebozos* from Mexico, *mantas* from Peru, *mei tais* from China, and *amautis* from Alaska.

Rather than stereotypical multicultural costumes, consider using "imagination fabrics" that are representative of the clothing used in different countries. The fabrics can inspire children to use their imagination to create their own costumes. Beautiful textiles from Guatemala, Peru, and Mexico can inspire children to create tablecloths, blankets to wrap a baby doll, or dresses and skirts. Saris from India can be made into veils, hair wraps, and capes. Scarves in different colors and designs can become rivers or lakes, can be used as hammocks, and can be used to transport other items. Re-create spaces that are common in children's daily living experiences to help children gain a sense of belonging and to build trust among all members of the classroom community.

CHAPTER 7
Cooking Spaces

In most cultures, eating food is a comforting and enjoyable experience. In some families, cooking time is a shared activity, while in other families, cooking is undertaken more as a chore. There are families who cook outdoors and families who cook in small indoor spaces or in large collective kitchens. Because of the diverse groups of children entering early childhood programs, educators need to be sensitive to all children when they design their cooking spaces.

Aesthetics: Beautiful elements can create inviting cooking spaces. Consider adding attractive nonbreakable dishes that are designed to represent ceramics from around the world. Include dish towels and napkins to match the dishes. Select a colorful tablecloth made of woven fabrics from Mexico, and place a centerpiece of bright, multicolored decorative balls. Bring in homelike elements, maybe a sign that says, *La Cocina es el Corazón del Hogar* (The Kitchen Is the Heart of a Home), to invite children to feel comfortable and safe. Peltre pots and pans (enamel cookware) and wooden spoons in different sizes, combined with natural loose parts, such as acorns, seedpods, and dried peach pits, can help children pretend to make soup or stews.

Authenticity: When designing cooking spaces, add authentic tools used by different cultures. Children can engage in pretend cooking as they represent everyday moments they experience in their families. Children may enjoy symbolically representing the way their families cook. For a Vietnamese child, a wok may be a necessary tool for cooking, while for a Mexican child, a tortilla press is a familiar tool. For some families from Caribbean countries, a mortar and pestle is a common tool in the kitchen. We consider these authentic tools to be loose parts because we have observed children using them in a variety of ways to represent their thinking. Change the loose parts, materials, and tools in the cooking space to represent the different cultures in the classroom. Jacaranda pods can be a great ingredient for pretend cooking. Children can use glass stones and pretend they are soap bubbles to wash their dishes. Soft felted balls can be used as pretend dim sum. Pebbles can be made into stews, and clay can be flattened with an Indian rolling pin, or *belan*, to make *chapati* bread. The possibilities are as varied as the diverse group of children in a program.

Equity: When early childhood programs are based on the concepts of fairness, equity, and inclusion, children develop empathy and the ability to nurture others. For instance, when the children noticed that Joel, who has a developmental delay, was struggling to use the chopsticks, they had the idea to ask families to bring chopsticks that would be easier for Joel to manipulate. This opened the opportunity for families to problem solve different ways to adapt a cooking utensil to support Joel. The children created the conditions for Joel to be included in their play and promoted equity and inclusion by engaging in social action.

Dynamic: The dynamic nature of loose parts can increase children's curiosity and support their play. Children enjoy making concoctions. Kitchens provide ample opportunities to explore and create mud cakes and pies decorated with maple seeds or beautiful bougainvillea flowers. Children can grind aromatic spices with dynamic tools from around the world: mortars and pestles of different sizes, metates made of volcanic rock, stone grinders, and wood bowls and mallets. Setting a play cooking space both indoors and outdoors is the perfect way for children to learn about how people from around the world prepare and cook their meals.

Praxis: Praxis includes understanding a theory of how children learn through play and offering practical opportunities for children to do so when practicing cooking and other daily tasks. One aspect of your praxis could focus on the process of using dramatic play to enhance sociocultural exchange among children. This begins with the invitation to include every child's voice and ideas. When children engage in dramatic play, they are incredibly capable of negotiating their cultural and social knowledge as they learn from each other. Gi, who is from Korea, was excited to show his friends the Korean eating area set up by the educators and his family. He explained that everyone had to take off their shoes and sit on the pillows. Gi started to show other children how to pick up small stones using chopsticks. The children spent time manipulating the chopsticks and learning about the different plates and bowls Gi's family brought into the environment.

Critical Reflection: Using critical reflection when designing cooking spaces can help children feel comfortable and engage in imaginative play. Reflect on and analyze any item you place in the environment: Does the environment reflect children's culture? Are the tools used in the cooking space familiar to most children? How will you introduce new tools and loose parts to children? These few questions can help guide your practices. For example, Miriam is from Mexico, and she values its colorful landscape and the culinary experiences. In one classroom, she brought in a *molinillo*, a wooden whisk stirrer traditionally used to make hot chocolate in Mexico. She introduced the *molinillo* during group gathering and shared her memories and traditions. She then invited children to share a cooking tool used in their family.

Yum! I Am Making Pozole

At Cheri Quishenbery's Family Care, the mud cooking space is a favorite spot where children gather to experiment making different concoctions. Mia enjoys making different food and is often seen in the mud cooking space. Many of the concoctions she makes are based on the food she eats at home. She has made pozole using pebbles to simulate the hominy used in the soup. She mixes mud and takes large leaves to pretend she is making tamales and tacos. By using loose parts, she is spending time representing her culture in an authentic way. She is going beyond the multicultural and stereotypical plastic food into further understanding and is representing her cultural values.

Tools and utensils that are familiar to children validate their culture and support them in engaging in more complex imaginative play. Children find pleasure in pretending to make food that they eat at home.

A Korean table is set with authentic dishes and utensils for Gi to share how her family eats at home.

CHAPTER 8
Imaginative Play

Children's play has been recognized as the major agent in young children's development and learning. Through imaginative play, children's imagination soars, their language expands, and their social skills develop. Swiss clinical psychologist Jean Piaget saw play as the way children learn and make sense of the world around them. He observed a significant relationship between cognition and social development. He also asserted that it is through peer interactions that children come to understand that other players have different points of view and perspectives than their own. Play, for Piaget, provides children with opportunities to develop social competence through ongoing interactions. Piaget stressed the idea that just as children construct knowledge (cognition), they also construct social knowledge. Social knowledge is the last and most complex type of knowledge that children learn to acquire. Piaget recognized that learning happens because of the interaction between children and their environment. He asserted that children cannot learn unless they are constantly interacting with their environment by testing and either confirming or disapproving their ideas. Knowing this important information, early childhood educators recognize the significance of a well-designed environment in supporting children's growth and development (Beloglovsky and Daly 2015).

Through pretend and symbolic play, children expand their vocabulary and make connections between an object and what the object is called. This is an important step toward reading and writing. Imaginative play allows children to communicate in their home language and supports children in learning another language. The following play sequence demonstrates how using their home language allows children to engage in complex play.

Luis is sitting on the floor surrounded by blocks, stones and craft sticks. As he builds a plane he says, "*Este es un avión para que mis abuelos me visiten*" (This is a plane for my grandparents to visit me). Listening to Luis, you know he has full command of Spanish. Throughout the year, Luis started combining a few words in Spanish with a few words in English. By the end of the year, Luis was effectively communicating in both languages. Communicating in their home language helps children to make a smooth transition into learning another language without losing their primary language.

Imaginative play also helps children develop convergent and divergent thinking and develop flexibility in shifting between different thoughts (Russ 2004). Both types of thinking abilities are important processes in children's understanding of diverse perspectives. Convergent thinking includes idea analysis, such as taking ideas, thinking about them, and making decisions. For children, this can mean developing an understanding of physical differences and figuring out who they are. Divergent thinking is comprised of idea generation and broadening one's perspective to come up with unusual and extraordinary ideas (Guilford 1973). For children, this may mean finding various ways to interact with diverse groups of people, such as finding a creative solution for a child who wants to join the restaurant play that is happening in the dramatic play area but cannot sit at the play table. Through role play, children explore different viewpoints by using convergent thinking (collecting concrete information) and divergent thinking (generating new ideas), and then transforming information into mental representations that they use to understand different perspectives.

Aesthetics: Use an aesthetic lens to move beyond narrow constructions of curriculum and learning environments. To engage children, infuse beautiful artifacts and loose parts that children can use in imaginative play. Provide children with the opportunity to engage in aesthetic experiences that appeal to their curiosity. Nature provides remarkably beautiful backgrounds in which children can explore, investigate, experiment, and play. Infuse a variety of natural loose parts for children to use in their imaginative play and spontaneously design their own plan for learning. Natural loose parts are not only beautiful, but children can use them in imaginative play: acorns can become food, pinecones can represent a car, a piece of driftwood can be a canoe—the possibilities are endless.

Authenticity: When materials are authentic, they can draw children into deep play and make them feel that they can stay awhile and wonder about how things work and how people live. To preserve authenticity, invite families to bring unique and interesting materials from home. Ask for loose parts that can be repurposed. They can be nature collections, cooking utensils, or tools that reflect the families' cultures. For instance, when a new law banned plastic bags from the stores in our state, children started talking about it. The educators along with the families collected bags and baskets from around the world. Children used the bags in their imaginative play to transport and carry items they "bought."

Equity: Children can learn about equity in their imaginative play by practicing collaboration and conflict resolution. Begin to promote equity by setting up a loose parts provocation that promotes imaginative play. Loose parts offer children opportunities to negotiate and solve problems together, which includes learning about equity. This is the beginning of acquiring moral values and a deep sense for equity. For instance, the older children in a mixed-age classroom may have learned that younger children do not know "the rules" and may knock over other children's block structures. Older children can understand that it takes time to learn the rules, and they can help the younger children learn them. This is the beginning of understanding the concept of equity.

Dynamic: The dynamic nature of loose parts can help children take risks, which is necessary as children learn about other cultures. It takes a risk to step into someone else's shoes and learn about who they are. There is a risk of rejection and the risk of meeting someone new. Children need to step out of what is comfortable in order to learn about different views and perspectives. When children pretend play with loose parts, they are free to take risks and test new ideas. When educators, children, and families work together to take care of the hazards, children are free to take risks and build confidence. Infusing fabrics, sashes, ribbons, and rope gives children the opportunity to change and transform into different characters from their imagination.

Praxis: Cultural praxis is created when educators know the children in their program. Knowing children's ideas, interests, and cultural values helps educators to create environments that engage children in imaginative play that supports their identity and promotes social development. Louise Derman-Sparks believes that it is important to look at classroom environments through a critical lens to determine messages about diversity that children receive from the materials and furnishings. Children get messages not only from what is there but also from what is not there. If, for example, my race, ethnicity, ability, or gender is not represented, I feel insignificant. We need to be thoughtful in designing settings based on specific cultural backgrounds of the children and families who are part of our school community. When the classroom is full of possibilities for exploring cultural diversity, children can develop to their fullest potential. It is important to provide materials that accurately reflect diverse populations (Derman-Sparks 1989).

Critical Reflection: Through critical reflection, educators can gain a deeper cultural understanding. Cultural sustainability involves strategic and intentional long-term planning that includes all components of an early childhood program. Critical reflection helps us plan to create a culture of trust where children feel a sense of belonging and comfort. Observing children's play and critically reflecting on their intention help educators to support children's understanding of the world. For instance, when children role-play about a sensitive issue, you can introduce a persona doll to help them understand their feelings. Powerful conversations among children occur as they discuss the stories that are inspired by each doll. A persona doll is a life-sized doll that is culturally authentic and has distinctive characteristics concerning such things as sex, ethnicity, body type, and ability. When educators listen to how children engage with a persona doll and critically reflect on the next steps to take, they can further support children's play. Critical reflection can lead you to ask difficult questions and introduce sensitive situations, such as a parent in jail, same-sex marriage, or bullying, to help children respond to real-life situations. Add loose parts for children to engage the persona dolls in open-ended play. We often see children carry, walk with, and invite the persona dolls to dress up and transform into new characters in sustained play sequences.

It Is Not Fair!

Alberto is a child with Down syndrome. He enjoys knocking down block structures other children build. This has caused a lot of frustration because the children have worked hard in building great structures. Teacher Debbie introduces Emilia, a persona doll, to help the children understand how Alberto may take time to understand how to play with others. She reintroduces Emilia to the children: "Remember this is Emilia, and she has Down syndrome. She is very loving and affectionate but has a hard time controlling her behavior. Last week she had fun playing in the water table by throwing the water toys and splashing the water. The other children at the water table didn't like it and yelled at her. How do you think that made her feel?" This leads to a conversation about Emilia wanting to play but not knowing how to play and to realizing that playing was hard for her. When Debbie asks what Emilia could do, Marina says, "It's hard for Emilia to talk, just like Alberto. She throws things like Alberto does. I think it's because she wants to play." She suggests showing Emilia how to pour water "like this" and raising a hand and saying stop when she splashes water. Marvin adds, "I think

the children should invite her to play but not throw water." Nicole says, "She forgets the rules. We could make a sign to remind her." The persona doll helps reach and teach the children about Down syndrome and offers solutions that are beneficial to all learners in the classroom, thus creating a sense of equity and inclusion.

Adding bags, baskets, and boxes from around the world invites children to use them in imaginative play. Sophia takes some metal washers and adds them to a bag, pretending they are money. Joaquin picks up a box and adds some shells, pretending he is carrying food from the market. As they play, the children are finding differences and similarities in the variety of methods used in other cultures to carry food, money, and other familiar items.

Small worlds invite children to use their imagination as they learn about the different habitats that exist in the world.

Instead of stereotypical traditional costumes, add fabrics from around the world to the dress-up area.

CHAPTER 9

Nurturing, Empathy, and Caring

Young children experience their world through their relationships with families, community members, and other caregivers. Safe, nurturing relationships and environments help children build empathy and learn to care for themselves and others. Nurturing relationships help shape the development of children's physical, emotional, social, behavioral, and intellectual capacities, which ultimately affect their ability to nurture and care for others. To care and nurture other people, children need to build empathy. Humanist psychologist Carl Rogers (1995, 142) states, "Empathy means temporarily living in the other's life, moving about in it delicately without making judgments." Empathy is part of what makes us human and gives us the ability to care for and nurture each other. It is the foundation for moral and ethical development. In young children, empathy may be the ability to notice other people's feelings and respond with care and concern. In *Daring Greatly: How the Courage to Be Vulnerable Transforms the Way We Live, Love, Parent, and Lead*, Brené Brown (2012) says there is no right or wrong way of being an empathic person. Instead, empathy is simply about listening, holding space, and avoiding judgment. Through empathy, we communicate the powerful message "You are not alone" (Brown 2012). To nurture and to be caring and kind people, children need to develop empathy, which helps them understand other people's feelings and perspectives.

Some of the ways children learn to nurture are by playing with dolls, interacting with senior adults, and cooperating with children who have diverse abilities. A dramatic play area needs dolls that represent the families in your program. Include dolls of both genders as well as the major ethnic groups in the United States (African American, Asian, Hispanic, Middle Eastern, Native American, and Caucasian). Introduce dolls with diverse abilities and dolls that represent senior adults. By playing with dolls, children become aware of their own feelings and individuality. They are able to relate their common feeling to the feelings of others and respond in ways that they imagine are comforting to that person. Regardless of children's gender, when they hold, feed, and rock a baby doll, they are practicing being loving to others. Nurturing dolls helps children process important events in their lives, such as the birth of a sibling. In their play, children can take the opposite role, which allows them to see another's perspective. Giving children the chance to have some power and control in play allows them to try using these abilities in a safe way and to respect that other people also have the need for power and control.

Children also learn to nurture as they engage with older adults. Young children focus on physical attributes. They develop their ideas of older adults based on what they see. For example, gray hair, a cane, and a wheelchair are symbols that children use to describe older adults. Spending time with grandparents and other older adults who are active helps children understand that using a cane or having gray hair does not define a person's age. At Cheri Quishenbery's Family Care, children can interact with different adults. Cheri's husband, Frank, regularly spends time with the children. He plays tea party with them, spends time sorting and classifying loose parts, and also helps the children use tools to build their ideas. Frank has gray hair, but he is very active. The children have learned that not all senior adults are fragile or cannot walk. Because Frank is caring and gentle with the children, they are learning to nurture and care for people of different ages.

Aesthetics: People define the aesthetics of the environment they inhabit (Apps and MacDonald 2012). Nurturing environments integrate the cultural values of children. Environments that create a sense of belonging help children develop nurturing skills. Design homelike spaces that support social interactions and build empathy. When children feel safe and secure, they can learn to be kind to other children. Consider creating spaces infused with photos of the families, art, soft pillows, rugs, and plants. This type of environment can bring a sense of comfort to children and families. Incorporating colorful photographs of families nurturing babies may inspire children to explore nurturing their baby dolls. Placing books with photographs of families transporting their babies may entice children to carry the baby dolls through the day. A beautifully set small table invites children to engage in symbolic play. Teacher Cheri set up a beautiful table where the children could enjoy a tea party. There was a pretty tablecloth, napkins, and china. She added Hawaiian sea beans, metal balls, and wooden tiles. The children were very excited because they knew that they would be playing tea party with Frank. They came over to the table where Frank was sitting, and Addy started carefully pouring tea from the beautiful china teapot. Marlisa brought the wooden pieces and served Frank a "cookie." Other children joined, and they took time serving Frank. In this simple exchange, children learned to care for Frank and for each other.

Authenticity: When children are experiencing the addition of a baby to their family, they sometimes re-create caring and nurturing with baby dolls. After reading *A Ride on Mother's Back: A Day of Baby Carrying around the World,* by Emery and Durga Bernhard, the children started to role-play different ways to carry their babies. They created slings using authentic fabrics from around the world, such as *cambaya* fabric from Mexico. They wrapped the dolls around their body using indigo fabrics from Japan, and they practiced carrying a baby using a *khanga*, a type of colorful skirt from Africa. Children also tested *pareos* from Haiti and *mei tais* from China and a beautifully embroidered Hmong-style carrier. Incorporating other books on baby wearing, such as *Beloved Burden: Baby-Wearing around the World,* by I. C. van Hout, offered children the history of baby carriers. This investigation helped children process what it is like to have a new baby in the house and also learn about different cultural traditions about babies.

Equity: When we give children the opportunity to play and learn to nurture and care for each other, we are helping them learn about fairness and equity. Through play, children feel that their voice is heard and respected. By feeling appreciated, children begin to develop the capacity to listen to other people's feelings, ideas, and needs. They are then better prepared to open their minds to develop rules that represent the voice of the whole group. This is part of nurturing, empathy, and caring for each other.

Dynamic: Because loose parts are dynamic, they support children's imaginative play. This can be seen as children nurture baby dolls. As children pretend to feed their dolls using tree cookies, wooden maple rings, coasters, and glass beads, they may show what they know about caring and nurturing. Boxes, baskets, large baking pans, and crates invite children to make beds for their dolls and to connect what they know about how a baby in their family sleeps. It is in this type of play that children may begin to make sense of the world and gain understanding of their emotions. Understanding their feelings is an important part of learning to care for and nurture other people. The dynamic nature of loose parts supports children's ability to accept and be kind to people with disabilities. For example, adding canes, along with leg and arm braces that they can wear, helps children learn what it is like to have a disability. When children engage in an exploration and a child with diverse abilities is having a difficult time participating, invite children to help adapt the activity so that everyone can participate.

Praxis: Praxis happens when educators observe and gain an understanding of children's thinking. Based on their observation, they can act and support children in gaining deeper knowledge of the world around them. Young children may try to understand a challenging experience, such as losing their home, going through a divorce, or moving to a different place. When educators are aware of what is going on in children's lives, they can support children by giving them the opportunity to re-create similar situations in their play. In imaginative play, children can gain knowledge and process their feelings about the reality they are experiencing.

Critical Reflection: As educators, we can critically reflect on how children demonstrate empathy in their interactions with each other. Observing how children engage in nurturing their dolls can give educators insight into children's thinking. For example, three-year-old Alvin held a baby doll and carefully placed it in a crate. He covered the doll with a colorful embroidered napkin and walked to the kitchen pantry to look for something to feed the doll. As the educators observe, they can add loose parts, such as bottles of different sizes, different napkins, and a small pillow to further support Alvin's play. He spent time feeding and nurturing the baby doll and is quietly developing nurturing skills. Educators should slow down and observe, hear what the children have to say, and marvel at the fantasies they create. Only then can teachers truly offer children the opportunities they deserve.

My New Friend Has Two Mommies

Teacher Debbie is walking around the room when she hears Kylah and Abril engaged in a conversation as they have a tea party with their dolls. They both want to take the role of the mother and are arguing about it.

Kylah says to Abril, "We can't both be the mommy; there is only one mommy in the family."

Abril looks her in the eye and says, "Can too! I have two mommies."

Teacher Debbie approaches the girls and says, "Kylah, in your family you have a mommy and a daddy; in Abril's family there are two mommies." She continues to say, "There are different types of families, and what is important is the love family members have for each other."

The children go on to play, and teacher Debbie notices that they are both pretending to be the mommy, but each has different roles and responsibilities in their play. After some reflection and conversations with other teachers in the program, teacher Debbie decides to read a book during group meeting time that features a family with two mommies. She is also intentional in displaying photos in the classroom environment that represent different family constellations and invites all the parents in the program to create a collective "family collage" using loose parts.

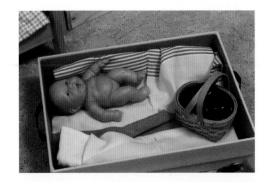

Alvin, Marlysa, and Addy are learning to nurture as they play with dolls. As the children explore baby beds from around the world, they are learning that nurturing is important, as well as something that happens in other parts of the world.

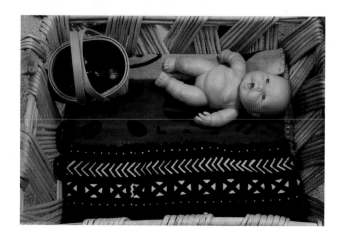

As the young children wash the dolls, they establish links between their action (washing the dolls) and their mental processes (the color of the baby doll's skin does not change with the water). Through this experience, children learn that skin color is permanent and it does not wash off. This helps them understand that people are born with certain skin colors, which is a unique physical characteristic. As children recognize that skin color does not wash off, they realize that many different people with different skin colors live and contribute to their community. Explorations about skin color help children learn to appreciate differences and find commonalities among them.

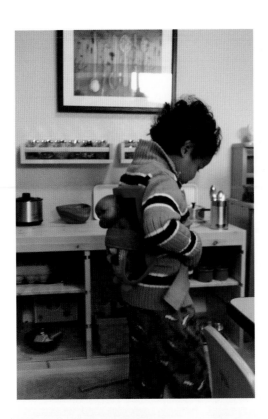

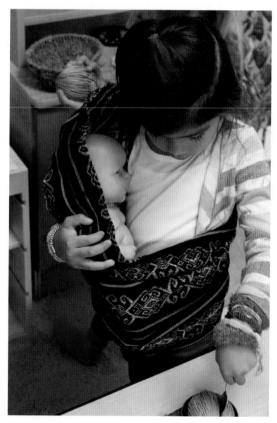

Part 5
Child, Family, Community

Child Identity

Community

Family

We live in a world in which we need to share responsibility. It's easy to say, "It's not my child, not my community, not my world, not my problem." Then there are those who see the need and respond. I consider those people my heroes. —FRED ROGERS

Children do not grow up in isolation. The moment children are born, they begin to develop a sense of who they are. Their identities are shaped by their family, educators, and community members alike. Today children are being raised by grandparents, aunts, uncles, and sometimes siblings. Each member of the family influences how children think and how they develop moral values. Harvard professor Jerome Bruner (1996) wrote, "culture shapes the mind, it provides us with the toolkit by which we construct not only our worlds but our very conceptions of ourselves and our powers." He goes on to say, "You cannot understand mental activity unless you take into account the cultural setting and its resources, the very things that give mind its shape and scope. Learning, remembering, talking, imaging: all of them are made possible by participating in a culture" (x–xi).

In *Other People's Children*, Lisa Delpit (2006) challenges educators to know themselves and their limitations, to know the children and families in their program, and to build honest relationships of mutual respect. Families and community members have important stories to tell and cultural values they can share with children. To honor children's cultures, it is important for the early childhood educators to form strong connections with each family that enters their program. By listening to families' stories and learning about their cultural values, educators can weave children's culture, language, symbols, heritage, and traditions into every aspect of the early childhood education programs. Why? Inviting families to be a part of the classroom community is crucial to support the social development of children.

When children see their parents participating in everyday activities, they know that the classroom is a place they can trust. Because trust and belonging are key components for learning and developing, children need an environment where they feel a sense of belonging, respect, love, and encouragement. Acknowledging children's feelings and fears can help them know that there are adults and peers who care for them. This creates a sense of trust and belonging. It is also important to help children develop a sense of pride in their family, friends, and community. Because children have a need to belong, it is important for educators to allow them to voice their ideas, their thinking, and their opinions. When children develop a sense of belonging and a strong connection with their family and community, they may become more resilient and emotionally healthy.

It is most important to create culturally sustainable environments where children, families, educators, and community members are filled with joy and wonder and where their identities are respected, cherished, and valued. Equity, justice, and inclusion are practiced in everyday interactions, and the focus is to promote a system where every child can flourish and every family can have access to the resources they need to support their children to become successful and contributing members of society. A culturally sustainable environment must be responsive to children's cultures and languages and represent their cultures with authenticity. A culturally sustainable environment is free of stereotypical images and a "tourist approach" that only showcases food, festivals, and traditional costumes.

There is no better example of how to create culturally sustainable environments than the ongoing integration of the Māori culture in the New Zealand early childhood educational system. In New Zealand there is respect for the Māori's sense of knowing and making sense of the world. The Māori culture has been woven into every aspect of the early childhood educational system. Every classroom integrates the Māori language, symbols, traditions, and values. Early childhood educators listen and respect the Māori views and make every effort to focus on empowering children. The physical environment represents Māori culture and traditions, which are reflected in the arts and design of the physical space. Stained glass, tile work, and other art media displayed in the environments are inspired by the sea and local flora and fauna. Educators in the centers represent the Māori culture and language and respect the unique and important values of the children. The Te Whāriki, or early childhood curriculum, is a framework that focuses on *tamariki* (children's) learning and development within a sociocultural context. The Te Whāriki underlines the importance of relationships between *kaiako* (teachers) and *whanau* (families). It emphasizes the learning partnership among educators, children, and families. Educators in New Zealand intentionally select meaningful activities for the children, such as *waiatas* (Māori folk songs), stories, and gatherings that have connections to Māori children's lives. Children learn from the natural environment and from the powerful Māori traditions. To respect the Māori ways of knowing, every program has a garden and open access to the outdoors. Children can spend time inside or outside as they choose, and both environments are designed to offer multiple possibilities for exploration. Spaces are inviting, and the community forms an integral part of the classroom environment. A *marae* (meeting grounds) is incorporated into many of the early childhood environments. In the Māori culture, a marae is a place to stand and belong, and it serves as a community gathering space for celebrations and meetings.

Culturally sustainable environments create a sense of community and provide opportunities to collaborate and learn from each other. Invite families to share their talents, such as painting, sculpting, woodworking, construction, and using different tools. Look for opportunities to invite families to work with children. By working together as a community, families get to know each other and share knowledge. The following story illustrates how families come together to support their children's interests.

. . . .

Alexis's father, Brandon, is an industrial designer. He comes to the program and starts building a block structure with the children. This goes on for a week. As the structure gets taller, he talks to the children about how to make the structure stable. At the end of the week, the structure reaches the ceiling. The children notice that there are not enough blocks to finish the structure. Maureen, Annie's mom, works with wood, so she brings a chunk of a wooden post left from building a gazebo. She helps the children learn to saw more blocks to add to the structure. The educators, along with the children, decide that more time is needed to finish the structure, so they change the daily schedule. When the structure is completed, the children, educators, and families plan a celebration. The children plan the menu, and the families gather to cook together. Matthew's mom, Susan, is a chef. She guides the children and families in cooking a delicious meal, which they all enjoy together.

To create a sense of community in your program, provide comfortable seating on porches and patios where parents can stay, talk with other parents, and observe their children while they play. Consider cozy chairs for reading books and for looking at documentation. Add tables where families can join their children in building or creating a work of art using loose parts. Every morning when Miriam dropped her children off at the center, their day began with outdoor experiences. Parents sat on benches around the sand area or on the stairs and engaged in conversation with each other as they watched their children play. There was a table with butcher paper for parents to draw, paint, or explore loose parts with children. These rituals provided a sense of community as parents got to know each other very well. Think of ways to invite parents into your school as their children transition into your program. You might provide a comfortable sofa where parents can relax and have a cup of coffee, or a rocking chair and photo album of children's important work for parents to view before beginning their day.

Another way of preserving the family is to invite them to share their traditions. Traditions are an integral part of family and school identity. Traditions create a sense of belonging, history, and continuity. They remind us of events that have shaped family, school, and community. Family traditions tell a story of family dynamics and interactions. Traditions and stories families share with children have a profound influence in the development of children's identity and self-confidence.

Add loose parts from the local community found during walks with the children. If your program is in the city, visit local stores and business owners. They may provide a wealth of loose parts, such as metal washers, wood scraps, wooden frames, and acrylic tubing. If your program is near nature, collect leaves, rocks, sticks, and other wonderful treasures and bring them into the classroom. Take photos of local landmarks, buildings, and other places with which the children are familiar. Display the photos for inspiration, and add loose parts for children to re-create their favorite landmark or building. Invite local artists and musicians to share their work with the children.

May is a tile artist in Southern California. She enjoys teaching the children about the beautiful tiles she works with, and gives children the opportunity to explore different designs. May takes some of the children's work and frames it so it can be displayed in the classroom. When community members such as May are invited to participate in the program, children realize that they are part of something bigger than themselves and learn to respect and appreciate the cultural values of their community.

CHAPTER 10
Children's Identity

Identity begins to develop at birth as children recognize a self-concept based on their abilities, gender, values, race, ethnicity, and language. Early on they define themselves in terms of specific labels, such as by gender, "boy" or "girl"; by physical characteristics, "tall" or "short"; or by the color of their skin, "black" or "white." You can support children in understanding and developing their identities in your classroom by adding familiar loose parts from home, using their home languages, and allowing them to use it in multiple contexts. Culturally sustainable environments that embrace and support children's unique identities can promote children's positive self-concept. Include loose parts and materials that invite children to come together with others, to interact, and to problem solve.

Aesthetics: In a culturally sustainable environment, children can learn to appreciate the aesthetic values of different cultures. Add self-portraits of famous artists from around the world, and invite children to create their own self-portraits using a variety of loose parts. Children will learn to appreciate the beauty of art and at the same time explore important components of their own identity. Aesthetic experiences give children the opportunity to explore what they like and dislike. Because children use their senses to explore the world, consider introducing a variety of loose parts that engage their senses. For instance, introduce mortars and pestles, and let them grind aromatic spices from different countries. Consider giving children the opportunity to use their sense of sight by exploring stained glass art from different countries. Include photos and books about stained glass in combination with loose parts such as glass beads and glass tiles so that children can explore light and color. As children learn about the aesthetics found in their environment, they may begin to recognize their own interests, characteristics, ideas, and capacities. These are all important parts of children's identity. Yoli and Mateo were standing in front of the light projector. They were mesmerized by the beautiful colors in the water bottles. They moved around the room exploring how the colorful shadows reflected off their bodies. Yoli started laughing and told Mateo, "Look, now you have blue hair." In return Mateo told Yoli, "You have red hair." The two of them spent more time exploring different colorful items on the light table. The conversation led to comparing other physical characteristics. In this exploration Yoli and Mateo recognized who they are and what they can do.

These powerful activities expose children to the beauty of light and help them explore their own identity.

Authenticity: Introduce authentic tools and materials into the environment. Authenticity brings a sense of being and belonging into early childhood environments. Educational theorist John Dewey argued that giving children the opportunity to explore real carpentry tools allows them to gain an understanding of their abilities and skills. Real hammers, saws, screwdrivers, and wrenches can give children confidence in their abilities and allow them to make connections with important people in their culture who use similar tools. The foundation for gender identity formation gets established during the preschool years (Derman-Sparks and Edwards 2010, 91). One of the ways educators can support children's gender identity development is by offering both boys and girls opportunities to explore roles traditionally assigned to members of a specific gender. For instance, as both boys and girls use real tools, they begin to develop a positive view of their gender. They also realize that both boys and girls have the power to use real tools.

Equity: In culturally sustainable classrooms, equity helps children know that the adults in their life believe in them. Equity is not about treating all children the same. Instead, it is about achieving equal outcomes by individualizing support for each child. Educators need to recognize the inequities of practices that require every child to act the same way or create the same craft. Instead, they need to create environments that represent all children and promote equity and inclusive practices. One area in which you can practice equity is in using children's names and surnames. You can acknowledge that children have the right to their names as part of their identities. Think about what your name means to you. Were you named after a loving family member or an important event? Our names may tell where the stars were at our birth or our families' hopes for the future. We are all unique, and so is our name because it is tied to our identity. A child's name and surname tell people who they are and that they belong to a family. Their name differentiates them from others; thus, a child will be recognized as an individual with feelings, thoughts, and ideas. Through their names, children become part of the history of their family and community. To support children's identity, consider placing rocks with letters painted on them into the environment to encourage children to explore the letters in their names. Adding a photo of a child's name created with the rocks engages that child in learning to recognize her name and connect it to who she is. Equity is created because every child can engage in the exploration at her own pace, her own ability, and her own interest instead of having to follow a prescribed curriculum that results in the same outcome for all children.

Dynamic: Loose parts give children the opportunity to represent who they are and to explore their diverse characteristics. Consider adding mirrors for children to look at themselves and notice the details that make them unique. Covering tubes and boxes with polyester film creates surfaces for children to see their reflections. Add dynamic loose parts, such as lenses from old eyeglasses, buttons, beads, and small tree cookies. Offer children the opportunity to create self-portraits that can be changed as children continue to explore their identities. As children use the mirrors to explore who they are, they show that they know their strengths and abilities. As children engage in these dynamic interactions with the mirrors, they develop a strong sense of belonging to the classroom community that further supports children's identities.

Praxis: When educators work to understand how children develop their identities and sense of self and use this important knowledge to create explorations that support identity development, they are engaging in cultural praxis. One aspect of identity development concerns race and skin color. Since we know that children notice racial differences at a young age, we want children to learn to value the uniqueness of each individual. Listen to how children describe themselves and each other. Do they make comments about some skin color being better than another? Because you want children to feel confident and secure within their own identities, use your observations to further support children's identities and to diffuse negative stereotypes and biases that may affect children's perceptions of self and others. Consider setting skin color explorations using ceramic tiles in different shades. Give children the opportunity to compare their own skin color with the skin color of other children in the program. Invite children to describe themselves and others with admiration and respect. Describe the ways in which children are unique and why this is important. Invite families to explore their physical attributes with the children. To continue the exploration, add skin color paint for children to mix until they are satisfied that the paint matches their own skin color.

Critical Reflection: Through critical reflection, early childhood educators contribute to the identity development of children. Critical reflection helps educators to understand their own practices and how to best support children's unique abilities and capacities. Critical reflection gives educators a starting point to understand individual children. You are better able to support children's individual identities when you ask yourself reflective questions, such as, Who are the children in my program? What knowledge do they bring? How can I best support them? For example, add materials such as mirrors and clay to explore skin colors. The educators at Loomis Head Start observed that children were comparing and contrasting their physical characteristics. To further support the children's understanding of differences and similarities, the educators set up a provocation with dolls made of different skin-colored fabrics, which are designed so that children can change the doll's physical characteristics. Fabrics from different countries, sashes, and ribbons for children to dress the dolls were added along with yarn hair that differed in color, length, and texture. This became a very engaging exploration for both boys and girls, who spent a long time changing dolls' hair color and using fabric to create outfits and hair scarves. As they played with the dolls, children talked about the different fabrics and made connections to their homes. Rose picked up a doll, dressed her, and added fabric to the doll's hair to look like a hijab, a head covering worn in public by some Muslim women. She showed us the doll and exclaimed, "This is Rose."

How Many Teeth Do You Have?

When we visit Loomis Head Start, we notice that a group of boys are playing with mirrors and loose parts with reflective surfaces. The children explore their identities as they investigate a variety of reflective items. First, Jacob, Genaro, and Ian start building a tower using the mirrored blocks and the silver Mylar bowls. They enjoy looking at their distorted images in the bowls. Laughter can be heard as they compare their eyes, noses, and mouths. Ian picks up a mirrored tray, opens his mouth, and exclaims, "Look, I have a hole where my tooth used to be." Genaro picks up another tray and looks inside his mouth and says, "Look, I lost a tooth." Jacob joins them, and they start comparing and counting how many teeth each of them has lost. This becomes an investigation of similarities and differences that encourages children to recognize that we are unique, yet we also share some characteristics. For example, we all have eyes, but they are different colors. We have different skin colors, but they are all beautiful.

Loose parts combined with real tools give children a sense of power and the confidence that comes from accomplishing a complex task.

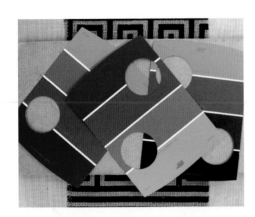

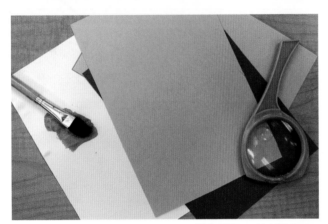

Loose parts give children the opportunity to represent who they are and to explore their diverse characteristics.

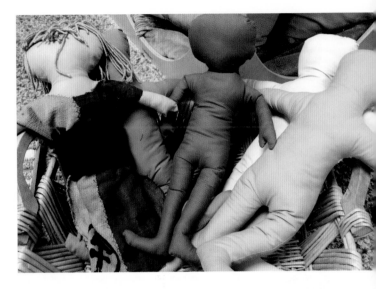

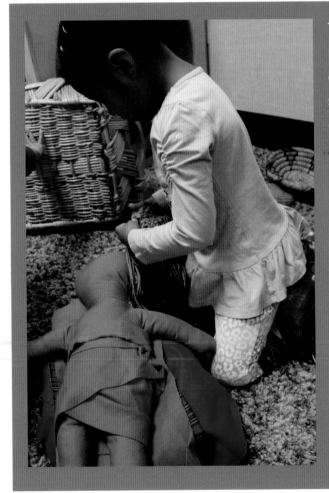

To support the children's understanding of differences and similarities, the educators set up a provocation with dolls made of different skin-colored fabric, which are designed so that children can change the dolls' physical characteristics. Fabrics from different countries, sashes, and ribbons for children to dress the dolls were added along with yarn hair that differed in color, length, and texture.

Jolette and Luz are working on a puzzle made of nonbreakable mirror pieces. As they put the pieces together, they are fascinated by their own reflections. Mirror play reinforces self-identity and helps build relationships as the girls compare and contrast each other's images.

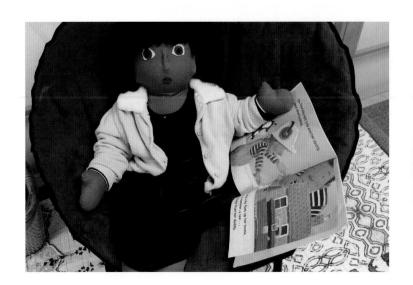

Teacher Jenna walks into the classroom with a visitor. The children run to greet them. Rose asks, "What is his name?" Teacher Jenna answers, "What would you like his name to be?" Rose says, "Walker. He is like my friend who wears something in his ear and can't walk." Walker, a persona doll, becomes a welcome visitor to the classroom.

CHAPTER 11
Family and School Traditions

Traditions are stories, beliefs, rituals, and customs that are passed from one generation to the next. Children find great comfort in the rituals they share with their families. Our daily routines and special occasion traditions also provide a sense of continuity for children year after year. Traditions connect the past, present, and future and give children and families a sense of history and respect for their heritage. Traditions are important because they help children make connections to their family's history and heritage. When educators invite families to share their traditions, they are honoring the important cultural values of each family.

Early childhood programs can build traditions to create and sustain a sense of community among children, families, and educators. Implementing traditions in early childhood programs can also bring a set of challenges for educators in, for example, the "holiday dilemma." Holidays can bring pleasure to many children, families, and educators, but they can also make other children feel excluded or isolated. Implementing family traditions and creating school and community traditions require intentionality and careful consideration of the diversity in the classroom. Instead of focusing on the materialistic aspects of traditions, invite families to share the gift of time in the classroom community. Encourage families to share their family history and cultural heritage. Work as a community to establish school traditions that create a rhythm and sense of connection. Another way to preserve traditions is by using photography and videos to record special moments that take place daily in the classroom. Do not limit traditions to specific times of year; instead, include traditions year-round. Invite children, families, and community members to plan and facilitate developmentally appropriate and culturally responsive traditions.

Aesthetics: Children need to be surrounded by beauty. Early childhood educators can design environments that promote the aesthetic values of the children's culture and community. As children are invited to explore loose parts to create art and to design, they learn to appreciate and judge the aesthetic values of their culture. In *The Aesthetic Imperative: Relevance and Responsibility in Arts Education*, author Michael Ross (2014) writes, "Aesthetic perception involves the capacity to respond to the uniqueness, the singular quality of things—to value individual integrity and to reject the cliché and the stereotype" (158). You can structure aesthetic experiences for children that are open-ended so children can create what is part of their imagination and thus express their feelings, knowledge, and cultural values.

Authenticity: As the U.S. population becomes more diverse, early childhood educators must find developmentally appropriate ways to respect children's cultures and traditions. The prevailing question is, How do we create environments that authentically represent children, family, and community? As educators, we need to recognize that a culturally sustainable environment goes beyond having an ethnic food celebration a couple of times a year and acknowledging a few well-known historical figures. As an early childhood educator, you have the opportunity and the responsibility to create environments that are inclusive and authentic and celebrate children's unique family histories and traditions. Consider the following ideas to help you incorporate authentic traditions into your program:

- Invite families to share their family traditions, and encourage the children to find similarities in the different family celebrations. Read about different cultures and about the specific values of each family.

- Educate yourself about the different cultures in your program.

- Research community traditions and the meaning behind the traditions. Use more than one source to gather information.

- Avoid "tokenizing" children. Do not put children on the spot to answer questions about their culture. Each child is an individual, and their experiences may or may not be like that of the group they represent.

Equity: One way to promote equity for all children is to provide opportunities to explore nature. Research shows that children benefit from being in contact with nature. In *Last Child in the Woods*, Richard Louv (2008) discusses the impact of nature deprivation on children's learning and development. Nature encourages children to explore how their bodies move, to use their senses, to be empathic and care for themselves and others, and to play and enjoy recreational activities. Nature introduces children to the idea that they are not alone in this world and that instead they are part of something larger than themselves. Offering children opportunities to access nature has become an issue of equity. Early childhood environments need to offer all children, regardless of geographical location, access to natural spaces. Providing loose parts in natural environments can offer children the opportunity to develop school and community traditions. For example, at Roseville Community Preschool, after the holidays families and educators gather Christmas trees. During break, they plant the trees in the outdoor environment. When children return to school, a forest of trees welcomes them. Loose parts, such as pinecones, beautiful crystals, rocks, and wood pieces, are available throughout the outdoor and indoor spaces, and children freely integrate them into the forest. The smaller loose parts are hung on the trees. Larger loose parts become obstacle courses that go through the forest. This is not only a wonderful tradition, it is also a valuable way for young children to work together and to share stories about the holiday season and their family traditions. The trees last a long time, and they are then recycled into tree cookies and tree stumps. By recycling the trees, children also learn positive traditions in sustaining their local environment.

Dynamic: Loose parts can engage children in learning about themselves and other children in their school and community. Loose parts also help develop a memory of the past, present, and future that sustains children and families. At Roseville Community Preschool, children gather at the end of the year and create a memory box. They select from a variety of loose parts to add to their memory box. This is a way to provide all children the opportunity to re-create a memory that was meaningful to them using adaptable materials that can hold a variety of meanings in each child's box. This is an excellent way to continue children's exploration of dynamic loose parts when they leave the program.

Praxis: The praxis of traditions and daily rituals happens when children, families, schools, and community members share knowledge and apply it to their daily interactions. In other words, praxis is the process of educators, children, and families coming together to share ideas and plan how to implement them. Meaningful traditions require planning and respect and the commitment of everyone involved. In *Teaching to Transgress*, American scholar bell hooks (1994) says that when educators create holistic environments, where educators learn along with the children and families, they are implementing a pedagogy of freedom. This type of pedagogy empowers children, families, and educators to learn about others and celebrate differences and similarities, while empowering children to engage in the process of decision making about what is important to them (hooks 1994).

Critical Reflection: The more time educators spend reflecting, the more they will be able offer children experiences that strengthen their practices. Reflection time is standard practice at the Center of Gravity, a child development center in Pleasant Hill, California. Their center staff wanted to provide an innovative, meaningful, and collaborative event to bring families together.

After thoughtful consideration, they decided to hold a celebration of light, an opportunity for their family community to come together and explore light with fascinating loose parts. After the event, the teachers critically reflected on what worked or what needed to change to make the celebration more inclusive. The educators concluded that children need to have positive and accurate experiences about human differences and similarities. These experiences may offer children the foundation for resisting combative, incorrect, and harmful messages that impact their identity and the identity of other people. Young children can develop critical thinking skills and the capacity to recognize what is fair and what is not. Critical reflection helps educators to cultivate children's empathy, recognize and avoid stereotypes, engage in social action, and recognize that unfairness hurts. Critical reflection helps educators to select loose parts that allow children to share a sense of place with adults and other children.

The Light That Brings Us Together!

The educators at the Center of Gravity, along with the families, want to move away from traditional holiday celebrations. They want to create a tradition that will bring families together in celebrating their shared values. After conversation with children, families, and community members, they realize that almost every holiday has an element of light. During Christmas, families add lights to their homes. Hanukkah is known as the festival of lights when Jewish families light candles for eight days. During Kwanzaa, the celebration of harvest, a *kinara*, or seven-space candleholder, is lit by families to represent the original stalk from which the African people originated. Lighting candles to honor the solar year celebrates the winter solstice. During Diwali, the Hindu festival of lights, houses, shops, and public places are decorated with small oil lamps called *diyas* and colorful lights. During the Islamic holiday of Eid al-Fitr, lights are put up in homes as part of the celebration that marks the end of Ramadan. After the conversation and decision-making process ends, the educators, children, and families decide to have a celebration of light that is inclusive of all children who attend the program. The children build with LED candleholders. They examine the way light

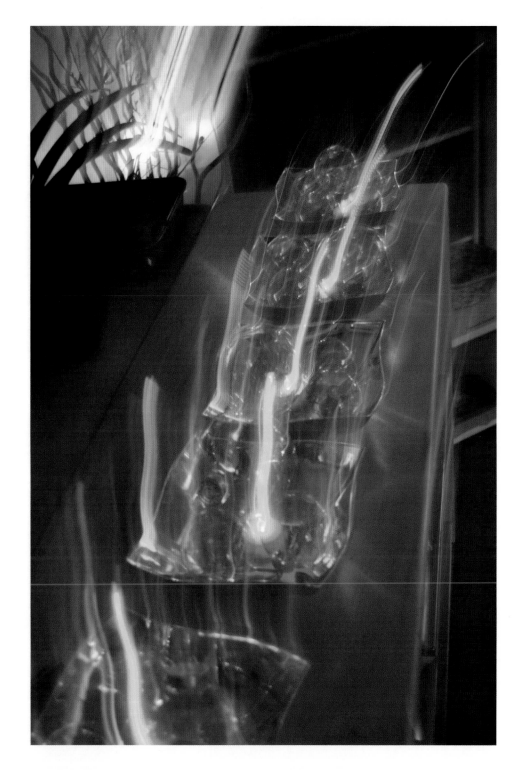

reflects off tubes covered with polyester film and investigate how light bounces off different clear and opaque loose parts. They explore light in water and look at paper snowflakes on the light table. The educators gather the children and families to sing and talk about how traditions bring people together.

When it is time to graduate from the program, children may have a hard time saying good-bye. They are leaving their friends, teachers, and a place where they feel comfortable. To ease the transition of changing schools, the educators at Roseville Community Preschool give children the opportunity to create a memory box with their favorite loose parts.

Tim Craig and his staff at Children's Circle Nursery School in Van Nuys, California, spend time critically reflecting on children's comments and interactions to create traditions that are meaningful to the children and families in the program. For example, the educators hide rocks and crystals throughout the outdoor environment. Children know that the rocks are buried, and they work together or alone to find them. Part of the tradition is that they can take home three rocks each week, and they must bury the other rocks they find for other children. By leaving rocks for others to discover, children are developing a sense of fairness.

Teacher Michelle introduces the children at the Center of Gravity lab school to her family's favorite game, Go. The children learn that Go originated in China and that it is the oldest game still played in its original form. The small stones fascinate Fin and Donovan, and they spend time lining them up on the wooden board. Games from different parts of the world can become an authentic way for children to learn about other cultures.

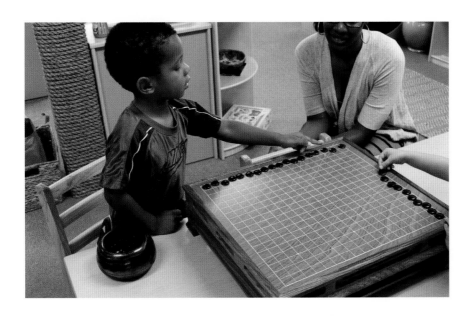

CHAPTER 12

Community

The knowledge and wisdom that a community holds collectively can enhance children's learning and healthy development. To engage families and community members in your classroom, begin by understanding each community's demographics, strengths, challenges, and concerns. It is important to start with an open mind. As much as you can, try to put your own assumptions and biases aside. Instead, invite families and community members to share their wisdom, interests, and hopes. Ask each family and community how they would like to be involved in your classroom. Learn about each other's histories and heritage. Respect and be responsive to diverse family constellations, structures, and dynamics. The most important thing is to bring a sense of humility and recognition that we are all part of a larger whole, and thus we have the responsibility to listen to, respect, and care for each other.

Aesthetics: Aesthetics in the community tell you a lot about the culture, interests, joy, passion, and hopes of its members. In *Art as Experience*, John Dewey argues that aesthetics in the environment help children develop an appreciation for beauty and help promote a higher level of cognition (Dewey 1934). In other words, when children spend time in an aesthetically pleasing environment, they may experience less stress, and they are able to spend more time pursuing their artistic and aesthetic interests. We venture to say that community aesthetics not only support cognition but also create a sense of well-being and belonging. The aesthetics of an environment help a community develop its identity. Children bring their community's identity and aesthetics with them into classrooms.

Authenticity: Authenticity brings children a deeper knowledge of their culture and the cultures of other children. Authentic explorations of art, cooking, and building can help children develop an understanding about other children's cultural values. Open-ended materials, such as loose parts, provide authentic possibilities for children to investigate, manipulate, design, and create items that are inclusive of different cultures. Children can manipulate loose parts in ways that are authentic to them.

In a conversation about Mexican people at school, children brought up mostly stereotypical comments about Mexico and its people. Diego interrupted the conversation and said that his grandfather was a famous artist who made Mexico beautiful, and not like what the children were describing. This led to an exploration of Byron Galvez,

Diego's grandfather, and a mosaic mural that he designed in Pachuca, Mexico, that visitors may touch as they walk the mural's length. This impressive work of art is considered the largest walking mural in the world. It is not only beautiful, but it is also dedicated to women and inspired by the women of the world. The children had an opportunity to explore photographs of the mural. Colorful ceramic tiles of different sizes were added to the environment. Children spent time arranging and designing the tiles into different configurations. In the process Diego gained a sense of pride, and the children learned to appreciate the authenticity of Mexican culture and the arts.

Equity: As educators focus on equity, access, and inclusion for all members of a program, they can create systemic change that comes from within the community. Children are capable of building community, which is the process of building relationships that help to bring people together around a common purpose, identity, and sense of belonging. By building community, members are accepted, and their unique characteristics are valued. This inclusiveness brings equity into the early childhood environment. When engaged in play with loose parts, children may find opportunities to negotiate, play together, learn from each other, and develop empathy. The more children play together in harmony, the more they learn to stand up for fairness and equity. Engaging families and community in the building of a large mural constructed with upcycled loose parts creates equity and further builds community relations.

Dynamic: The dynamic nature of loose parts invites families and community members to discover new items to bring into the environment that can both build and benefit community. Families can help collect loose parts when they go on walks in their communities, when they visit garage sales, or when they share found materials from their homes. Community members who have special skills and knowledge might provide wooden blocks, spools, and planks of different sizes, and even bricks leftover from construction sites. Purchase a few smooth-edge can openers that leave no sharp edges on cans or lids, and loan them to families to upcycle cans. Once you gather different-sized cans, add them to the classroom environment for children to use in construction and pretend cooking.

Praxis: When children, families, and educators exchange ideas through dialogue, they are creating a bridge to unify cultural knowledge and practices to strengthen the overall development of children. Use the knowledge you gain from children and families to incorporate children's home culture as an integral part of your learning community. These opportunities to share ideas help children create strong bonds with educators and other children in the classroom.

Critical Reflection: Educators need to take advantage of teachable moments and use critical reflection to strengthen children's identities. They need to give children the ability to explore differences and similarities and celebrate each other's strengths. Teachers should help promote children's self-exploration and self-reflection in play with loose parts and other engaging materials. Intentional teachers offer opportunities to play with loose parts that help children to admire and accept their sameness and uniqueness. They create learning communities in which they are all free to explore and analyze biases, celebrate diversity, and find common respect for each other.

The Gift of Community

Through integrating the community that lies just beyond our fences, we build on the children's personal experiences, further expanding their understanding and creating new connections with the world around them. At the University of California Santa Barbara Children's Center, educators have used their location near the Pacific Ocean to inspire creativity and the joy of discovery in a natural setting. Art installations by local artists reflect the flora, fauna, and geography of the

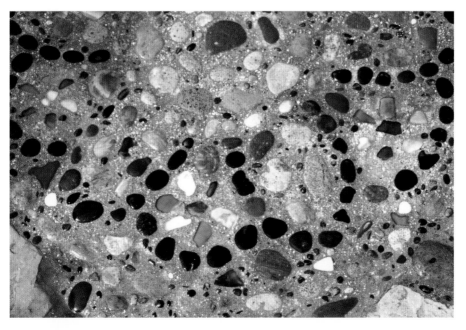

area, so children are immersed in multiple perspectives of their natural world. The materials the children use are found in the art, in the playscapes, and in the world beyond the center, inviting a deeper appreciation for the familiar and the novel possibilities therein. —Story shared by Leslie Vos and Annette Muse, University of California Santa Barbara Children's Center

Folsom Lake is one of the favorite spots in the community. Children know the lake, and they enjoy re-creating it using rocks and water in the sand area.

At Loomis Head Start, the children work together in a community garden. The educators, families, and children plant corn, sunflower seeds, and other vegetables. The children enjoy watering the plants. When it is time to harvest the crops, the children work together to gather the corn, and the educators cook it for lunch. The also grind some of the corn and sunflower seeds for feeding the birds. This is a great way for children to learn about sustaining their environment.

Community landmarks can serve as inspiration for long-term investigations. Lincoln, California, is home to the landmark Gladding, McBean ceramic factory. The factory produces beautiful ceramic pottery and terra-cotta work that is admired around the world. The factory's building brings a sense of history into the community. Children know the building and recognize that it is part of their community. For children to further explore the beautiful aesthetic values of the Gladding, McBean factory, educators introduced photos of the building and the pottery. They also offered children a variety of loose parts to use for construction, such as terra-cotta pots. This brings the aesthetics of the local community into the classroom and helps children become part of the surrounding beauty.

Appendix: About Our Advisory Committee

 **Kellie Cunningham Bliss, MA,** has been in the field of early childhood education for over thirty years, primarily as a classroom teacher. She pulls stories from her personal teaching experiences as well as from a parent's perspective. Being Native Alaskan and having lived in diverse cities, she brings insight and awareness to racial and cultural issues. She studied human development at Pacific Oaks College, where she received her master's degree. She currently teaches at the college level in Northern California.

 **Shawn Bryant** is the founding director and chief professional development officer of the Teaching Excellence Center in Oakland, California. He is an educational coach, facilitator, and consultant with over twenty-five years of educational experience in urban, suburban, and rural school districts and early-learning settings. Much of Bryant's work supports teachers, programs, and school and district leaders in planning and implementing large-scale improvement initiatives, visioning, understanding change and its effect on people, evaluating school improvement progress, designing exceptional professional development, and engaging people in productive, relationship-rich, results-based conversations with children and families at the core. A former Head Start teacher, Bryant has directed a NAEYC-accredited center, evaluated state universal prekindergarten, and managed county Head Start and state pre-K programs. He coaches and consults with teachers and instructional leaders.

 **Joyce Daniels** is an adjunct instructor in early childhood education and human development at American River College, Folsom Lake College, and Sierra College. She has taught and administered early childhood programs for more than thirty-five years in California, Virginia, Colorado, and Idaho. She received her bachelor's degree from Santa Clara University; elementary teaching credential from California State University, San Jose; and a master's degree in early childhood education from California State University, Sacramento. Daniels is an active member of several professional organizations, including the National Association for the Education of Young Children (NAEYC), the Center for Social Change, Peace Educators Allied for Children Everywhere (PEACE), and Educators for Peaceful Classrooms and Communities (EPPC). She has been a regular presenter at NAEYC and California Association for the Education of Young Children (CAEYC) conferences and has served as a reviewer for CAEYC conference proposals. Joyce has served as accreditation chair on the CAEYC board and has assisted programs in achieving accreditation and reaccreditation. She is the mother of two daughters.

 **Iris Dimond** was born in Chicago and is a longtime resident of California. Dimond has taught at Cosumnes River College for fourteen years as an adjunct and now as an associate professor. One of the things she shares with her students is that they should never forget the wonder and excitement of childhood; never forget how to play. Dimond is an accomplished ceramics artist and a community activist and leader. She dedicates her life to promoting the visual and performing arts and has been recognized for her volunteer and leadership efforts. She is passionate about promoting equity and teaching about culture and diversity in early childhood education.

 **Michelle Grant-Groves** is the founding director of the I.3 Institute: Inquiry, Intention and Innovation, an emerging early-education consulting cooperative dedicated to connecting and empowering the current early-care and education system, birth through third grade, and beyond. She is also the founder and executive director of the Center of Gravity, a STEM-based early childhood education lab school for the institute, located in Pleasant Hill, California. Grant-Groves's professional work is centered around designing community systems of practice that support racial justice and inclusion, and using inquiry and equity as core levers for authentic change and community transformation. She brings with her over twenty years of service in both the public and private sectors of early education, having served as a classroom teacher (infant through fifth grade), school-site and district administrator, worthy-wage advocate, author,

and now national professional development designer and facilitator. She holds a bachelor's degree in research and policy and in child and adolescent development; and a master's degree in early educational leadership; and she is currently pursuing her doctoral degree in educational leadership from Mills College in Oakland, California.

Michael Leeman is a teacher and director at Roseville Community Preschool. For over twenty-five years, he copresented workshops, seminars, and conferences with Bev Bos, his mentor, colleague, and mother-in-law. Leeman is a musician, author, and illustrator. Among his published works are *Morningtown Ride, Chants, Fingerplays and Stories,* and *Starting in a Corner,* a digital magazine for parents and teachers. He resides in Roseville, California, with his wife, Carrie, and their two daughters.

Lorraine Lima is a cocreator of curriculum for community health and social service transformative practitioners. She is a talented visionary leader and designs opportunities and possibilities for shifting current paradigms from "what is wrong" to "what is strong." Lima has a deep belief in the transformative power of connecting and cocreating community within circles. Currently, she is writing a children's book utilizing forest animals living along a river to demonstrate the importance of respect, forgiveness, and compassion. She is an artist in many mediums: watercolor, collage, acrylic paints, boxes, mandalas, masks, and canvas. Lorraine received a master's degree in human development and community service.

Cindy Linhares, MA, ED, has worked in a wide variety of service organizations in the infant, toddler, and early childhood field. Her areas of study include attachment, brain development, the power of play, and children who have special needs. Studying Magda Gerber's principles of respectful caregiving and observation skills in Budapest, Hungary, led to becoming a member of Resources for Infant Educarers (RIE). Linhares was a demonstration lecturer at the University of California Davis Center for Child and Family Studies, and has been an adjunct faculty member and lecturer at local community colleges. She has presented on infant and toddler development for various organizations and as a guest speaker for the Program for Infant/Toddler Care (PITC), where she has spoken on the topic of respectful caregiving for children with special needs. In addition, Linhares currently serves as a board member for Warmline Family Resource Center and is a core member of the Sacramento Area Infant Toddler Network.

 **Patrick Pieng** earned his Ph.D. in education with emphases in child and adolescent development and cognitive science from the University of California, Santa Barbara. His primary areas of research focus on children's development related to theories of mind understanding and emotion knowledge. He joined the Child Development faculty at California State University, Sacramento, in 2015.

 **Tu Bears** comes from a long, colorful line of characters in a soapbox novel, and her upbringing taught her to create rhythmic, bluesy song and dance riding across the wind. There was magic in every day. From before she could stand, the gift of ceremony was collected in her sturdy bones. Prayers, songs, and ritual were gently passed down in a deep connectedness to earth, sky, water, and wind. Every life form was respected and had purpose. In the world today, Tu Bears carries on as an author, poet, artist, and storyteller. She continues to be a lifelong student and practitioner of mysticism, metaphysics, and esoteric spiritual possibilities. Tu Bears is a coauthor of *Infinite Footprints*. Her writings have appeared in the anthologies *Reinventing the Enemy's Language* and *Women for All-Seasons* and in the magazine *Blue Mesa Review*.

 **Esther Villa** has over thirty-five years of experience in community organizing, parent advocacy, training facilitation, connecting resources, managing social service programs, and supervising staff. Her strengths are in collaboration, leadership facilitation, and community organizing. She has worked diligently with parents and guardians, as she believes that they are the key and the models for empowering children to reach their goals. She has focused her past twenty years in the Pacoima neighborhood in the San Fernando Valley. Villa is one of the founders of the nonprofit called Our Streets Dream–Nuestras Calles Sueñan. She is directing programs for youth and adult leadership and developing a promotora program that will eventually employ full-time promotoras with benefits. This is her dream. She is on her quest for financial support to make this dream a reality for the community.

Glossary

acceptance. Recognizing other cultures and acknowledging them as viable alternatives to one's own worldview.

accommodate. To offer kindness and support.

adaptation. To view cultural differences as a valuable resource while changing one's behaviors to the different cultural norms of one's environment.

aesthetics. A branch of philosophy that deals with the nature of art, beauty, and taste. It is a lens that allows us to look closely at the creation and appreciation of art, design, and beauty.

authentic environments. How children's history, values, and traditions are represented in early childhood learning spaces.

authenticity. The exchange among people that promotes, enhances, and sustains understanding, equity and equality, harmony, justice, and inclusion. It means that we learn from each other's history, individual experiences, traditions, values, and language as they exist within our own individual cultural context. Authenticity helps us avoid stereotypical and biased assumptions.

belonging. The act of becoming a member of something.

bravery. The act of speaking against injustice and discrimination. The ability to stand up for your beliefs.

commitment. Making a conscious decision to dedicate oneself to something, such as a person or a cause.

compassion. Loving oneself so that one may love another. Sometimes compassion is attached to sympathy for others.

connection. A bond or attachment usually through an emotional or mental state.

consistency. Maintaining motivation, follow-through, and expectation no matter what comes.

courage. The ability to face obstacles both small and large in the face of some fear.

creating. The act or moment of genesis within an idea, experience, or occurrence. To bring something into existence.

critical reflection. The ongoing process of consideration, analysis, and informed decision making that educators apply in their daily work with children, families, and colleagues. It is a necessary skill that leads to powerful change, helps us question our practices, and allows us to thoughtfully and intentionally respond and support children's learning, development, and culture.

culturally sustainable environments. Early childhood spaces that affirm children's cultural identity and reflect the culture, history, language, and traditions of the children, families, and community.

culturally sustainable pedagogy. Teaching that seeks to perpetuate and foster linguistic, literate, and cultural pluralism as part of the democratic project of schooling. This approach urges educators to actively value and preserve our multicultural and multilingual society while creating space for growth within and across cultures (Dancu 2014).

decision making. The action or process of making conclusions, especially important ones.

dignity. The innate human quality of being valued, honored, and respected irrespective of social rank, class, status, or "othering."

discernment. The ability to judge well.

discomfort. The feeling one has when confronting a circumstance, situation, or viewpoint that causes uneasiness. Culturally responsive thinking seeks to walk toward discomfort as a way of creating cultural brokering.

discovery. Learning about the world and how it works.

dynamic materials. Open-ended objects that can be physically manipulated and controlled by a child.

dynamism. The celebration of race, ethnicity, class, gender, sense of place, religion, and family that contributes to children's cultural identity. The nature of culture is dynamic as it shifts and changes with each group of children that enters a center program.

empathy. The internal capacity to understand or feel what another person is experiencing based on our shared humanity; perspective taking, placing oneself in the other's shoes to better understand his lived experience.

energetic. Being powerful in our actions, decisions, and interactions.

exploration. Traveling in or through an unfamiliar area in order to learn about it.

history. The study of past events, particularly in human affairs.

honesty. A moral attribute that indicates integrity, truthfulness, and straightforwardness.

honoring. Holding a person or value in high regard.

hopefulness. The capacity to be optimistic in everything we do. What we feel when we think life is worth living.

humility. Taking an active stand to hold someone else up; recognizing something without giving oneself recognition, praise, or acknowledgment.

identity. The attributes, abilities, attitudes, and values that we believe define us as an individual.

imagination. The ability to create that which is not from one's reality.

insightful. Having the ability to understand other people.

integration. Accepting that identity is not based in any single culture; instead, it is the ability to shift between different cultural frames of reference while maintaining one's own identity.

integrity. The quality of being honest and making personal choices with morality.

introspection. The ability to reflect and process one's internal mental and emotional state.

joyful. Expressing great pleasure and happiness.

kindness. An ethical disposition that characterizes true concern for another person's well-being.

listening. A choice to pay attention to what a person is saying.

magical. Beautiful or delightful in such a way as to seem removed from everyday life.

openhearted. The quality of expressing one's feelings honestly and with care.

openness. The ability to learn from others and respect diverse points of view.

patience. The ability to wait without criticizing or imposing one's own belief system.

perspective taking. The act of seeing someone else's understanding, views, beliefs, and values without judgment, while holding one's own understanding, views, beliefs, and values in the same regard. Perspective taking seeks to eliminate an either/or stance.

playful. Giving or expressing pleasure and amusement.

powerful. A sense of self-assurance and the ability never to hurt someone else for one's benefit.

praxis. Action informed by theory. Praxis is created as educators learn about the culture and language of the children in their program, and as they use this knowledge to guide their practices as they support children's identity, growth, and development. In other words, they apply theory.

provoking. Disruptive action, conversation, object, or element that causes disequilibrium, critical thinking, or self-regulation in oneself and others.

reflective. Having the ability to evaluate one's thoughts, feelings, and behaviors.

relationship. An alliance with or connection to other people or a value system.

respect. A feeling of deep admiration for someone or something elicited by their abilities, qualities, or achievements.

responsibility. A duty or obligation created by our own commitment to self and others.

risk taking. Using inborn and innate capabilities and capacities to challenge oneself against natural or man-made environments. Risk taking is a necessary approach to learning.

safety. The condition of being protected from harm and unnecessary risk.

sustainability. The capacity to support, uphold, or strengthen resources, values, culture, and traditions to ensure continuation for future generations.

sustainable. Having the ability to keep on going or to maintain a certain level of confidence.

thorough. Completeness in any form that offers a release.

thoughtful. Absorbed in or involving in contemplation. Showing consideration for the needs of other people.

trust. The process of exposing one's vulnerable self to others, while believing that they will respect one's openness. Both an emotional and a logical act, it happens as one logically assesses the possibilities of loss and gain based on the performance of other people. One might feel, "I trust you because I have experienced your trustworthiness and because I have faith in human nature."

understanding. The philosophical reasoning that allows us to grasp the good, from which wisdom, courage, temperance, and justice derive.

visionary. Having the ability to think about and plan for the future.

vulnerability. The quality or state of being exposed to the possibility of being attacked or harmed, either physically or emotionally.

References

Apps, Linda, and Margaret MacDonald. 2012. "Classroom Aesthetics in Early Childhood Education." *Journal of Education and Learning* 1, no. 1:49.

Bairaktarova, Diana, Demetra Evangelou, Aikaterini Bagiati, and Sean Brophy. 2011. "Early Engineering in Young Children's Exploratory Play with Tangible Materials." *Children, Youth and Environments* 21, no. 2:212–35.

Beloglovsky, Miriam, and Lisa Daly. 2015. *Early Learning Theories Made Visible*. St. Paul, MN: Redleaf Press.

Bernhard, Durga. 1996. *A Ride on Mother's Back: A Day of Baby Carrying around the World*. New York: Gulliver Books, Harcourt Brace and Company.

Bronfenbrenner, Urie. 1994. "Ecological Models of Human Development." In *The International Encyclopedia of Education*, 2nd ed., edited by Torsten Husén and T. Neville Postlethwaite, 3:1643–47. Oxford, England: Pergamon Press.

Brown, Brené. 2012. *Daring Greatly: How the Courage to Be Vulnerable Transforms the Way We Live, Love, Parent, and Lead*. London: Penguin Publishing Group. Kindle.

Bruner, Jerome. 1996. *The Culture of Education*. Cambridge, MA: Harvard University Press.

Chalufour, Ingrid, and Karen Worth. 2003. *Discovering Nature with Young Children*. St. Paul, MN: Redleaf Press.

———. 2004. *Building Structures with Young Children*. St. Paul, MN: Redleaf Press.

Charlesworth, Rosalind, and Karen Lind. 2012. *Math and Science for Young Children*. 5th ed. Clifton Park, NY: Thomson Delmar Learning.

Clements, Douglas H. 2004. "Major Themes and Recommendations." In *Engaging Young Children in Mathematics: Standards for Early Childhood Mathematics Education*, edited by Douglas H. Clements and Julie Sarama, 7–76. Mahwah, NJ: Lawrence Erlbaum Associates.

Curtis, Deb, and Margie Carter. 2003. *Designs for Living and Learning: Transforming Early Childhood Environments*. St. Paul, MN: Redleaf Press.

Dancu, Tony. 2014. *Culturally Sustaining Pedagogy: Expanding Culturally Responsive Theory and Practice: An ISE Research Brief Discussing Paris, Culturally Sustaining Pedagogy: A Needed Change in Stance, Terminology, and Practice."* Retrieved from http://relatingresearchtopractice.org/srticle/328

Delpit, Lisa. 2006. *Other People's Children: Cultural Conflict in the Classroom.* New York: The New Press.

Dengler, Marianna. 1996. *The Worry Stone.* Flagstaff, AZ: Northland Publishing.

Derman-Sparks, Louise. 1989. *Anti-bias Curriculum: Tools for Empowering Young Children and Ourselves.* Washington, DC: National Association for the Education of Young Children.

Derman-Sparks, Louise, and Julie Olsen Edwards. 2010. *Anti-bias Education for Young Children and Ourselves.* Washington, DC: National Association for the Education of Young Children.

Derman-Sparks, Louise, and Patricia Ramsey. 2011. *What If All the Kids Are White? Anti-bias/ Multicultural Teaching Strategies.* 2nd ed. New York: Teachers College Press.

Dewey, John. 1934. Art as Experience. New York: Perigee Books.

———. 1938. *Experience and Education.* New York: Touchstone.

———. 1987. *My Pedagogic Creed.* First published in *School Journal* 54, no. 3 (January 1897): 77–80.

Early Years Learning Framework for Australia. 2009. *Belonging, Being and Becoming.* Commonwealth of Australia.

Edwards, Carolyn P., and Linda Mayo Willis. 2000. "Integrating Visual and Verbal Literacies in the Early Childhood Classroom." Faculty Publications, Department of Child, Youth, and Family Studies. Paper 6. http://digitalcommons.unl.edu/famconfacpub/6.

Feeney, Stephanie, Doris Christensen, and Eva Moravcik. 2016. *Who Am I in the Lives of Children? An Introduction to Teaching Young Children.* Englewood Cliffs, NJ: Merrill.

Fox, Jill Englebright, and Robert Schirrmacher. 2015. *Art and Creative Development for Young Children.* 8th ed. Belmont, CA: Wadsworth.

Freire, Paulo. 1994. *Pedagogy of Hope.* London: Bloombury.

———. 1996. *Pedagogy of the Oppressed.* London: Penguin Books.

Gilbride, Shelly. *At the Crossroads of the Arts and Equity.* Pasadena: California Alliance for Arts Education. artsed411.org/files/arts.equity.f.pdf.

Gold, Zachery S., James Elicker, Ji Young Choi, Treshawn Anderson, and Sean P. Brophy. 2015. "Preschoolers' Engineering Play Behaviors: Differences in Gender and Play Context." *Children, Youth and Environments* 25, no. 3:1–21.

Gonzalez-Mena, Janet. 2008. *Diversity in Early Care and Education: Honoring Differences.* Boston: McGraw-Hill.

Gross, Carol. 2012. "Science Concepts Young Children Learn through Water Play." *Dimensions of Early Childhood* 40, no. 2:1–10.

Guilford, Joan P. 1973. *Characteristics of Creativity.* Springfield, IL: Illinois State Office of the Superintendent of Public Instruction, Gifted Children Section.

Hale, Christy. 2012. *Dreaming Up: A Celebration of Building.* New York: Lee and Low Books.

Hammond, Zaretta. 2015. *Culturally Responsive Teaching and the Brain: Promoting Authentic Engagement and Rigor among Culturally and Linguistically Diverse Students.* Thousand Oaks, CA: Corwin.

hooks, bell. 1994. *Teaching to Transgress: Education as the Practice of Freedom*. New York: Routledge.

Isadora, Rachel. 2010. *Say Hello!* New York: G. P. Putnam's Sons.

Kissinger, Katie. 2014. *All the Colors We Are: The Story of How We Get Our Skin Color*. St. Paul, MN: Redleaf Press.

Ladson-Billings, Gloria. 1995. "Toward a Theory of Culturally Relevant Pedagogy." *American Educational Research Journal* 32, no. 3:465–91.

———. 2009. *The Dream Keepers: Successful Teachers of African American Children*. 2nd ed. San Francisco: John Wiley and Sons, Inc.

Lee, Wendy, Margaret Carr, Brenda Soutar, and Linda Mitchell. 2013. *Understanding the Te Whāriki Approach: Early Years Education in Practice*. New York: Rutledge.

Louv, Richard. 2008. *Last Child in the Woods: Saving Our Children from Nature-Deficit Disorder*. New York: Algonquin Books. Kindle.

Machado, Jeanne M. 2016. *Early Childhood Experiences in Language Arts: Early Literacy*. 11th ed. Clifton Park, NY: Thomson Delmar Learning.

Martin, David. 2001. *Constructing Early Childhood Science*. Clifton Park, NY: Thomson Delmar Learning.

Maslow, Abraham. 1999. *Toward a Psychology of Being*. 3rd ed. New York: Wiley and Sons.

Moll, Luis C., Cathy Amanti, Deborah Neff, and Norma Gonzalez. 1992. "Funds of Knowledge for Teaching: Using a Qualitative Approach to Connect Homes and Classrooms." *Theory into Practice* 31, no. 2:132–41.

Murphy, M. Shaun. 2012. "Mathematics and Social Justice in Grade 1: How Children Understand Inequality and Represent It." In *Spotlight on Young Children: Exploring Math*, edited by Amy Shillady, 15–20. Washington, DC: National Association for the Education of Young Children.

National Research Council. 2002. *Investigating the Influence of Standards: A Framework for Research in Mathematics, Science, and Technology Education*. Washington, DC: National Academy Press.

Neuman, Susan, and Kathy Roskos. 1990. "Play, Print, and Purpose: Enriching Play Environments for Literacy Development." *The Reading Teacher* 44, no. 3:214–21.

———. 1997. "Literacy Knowledge in Practice: Contexts of Participation for Young Writers and Readers." *Reading Research Quarterly* 32, no. 1:10–32.

Nicholson, Simon. 1971. "How Not to Cheat Children: The Theory of Loose Parts." *Landscape Architecture* 62:30–34.

Nieto, Leticia, with Margot Boyer, Liz Goodwin, Garth R. Johnson, and Linda Collier Smith. 2010. *Beyond Inclusion, beyond Empowerment: A Developmental Strategy to Liberate Everyone*. Olympia, WA: Cuetzpalin Publishers.

OWP/P Architects, VS Furniture, Bruce Mau Design. 2010. *The Third Teacher: 79 Ways You Can Use Design to Transform Teaching and Learning*. New York: Abrams. Kindle.

Prairie, Arleen Pratt. 2005. *Inquiry into Math, Science, and Technology for Teaching Young Children*. Clifton Park, NY: Thomson Delmar Learning.

President's Committee on the Arts and the Humanities. 2011. *Reinvesting in Arts Education: Winning America's Future through Creative Schools*. Washington, DC: President's Committee on the Arts and the Humanities.

Ramsey, Patricia. 2004. *Teaching and Learning in a Diverse World: Multicultural Education for Young Children*. New York: Teachers College Press.

Robinson, Kerry H., and Criss Jones-Diaz. 2005. *Diversity and Difference in Early Childhood Education: Issues for Theory and Practice*. London: Open University Press

Rogers, Carl. 1995. *A Way of Being*. Boston: Houghton Mifflin Harcourt. Kindle.

Roskos, Kathy, and Susan Neuman. 1994. "Play Settings as Literacy Environments: Their Effects of Children's Literacy Behaviors." In *Children's Emergent Literacy: From Research to Practice*, edited by David F. Lancy, 251–64. Westport, CT: Praeger.

Ross, Michael, ed. 2014. *The Aesthetic Imperative: Relevance and Responsibility in Arts Education*. Oxford: Pergamon Press. Kindle edition.

Russ, Sandra W. 2004. *Play in Child Development and Psychotherapy: Toward Empirically Supported Practice*. Mahwah, NJ: Lawrence Erlbaum Associates.

Seo, Kyoung-Hye. 2003. "What Children's Play Tells Us about Teaching Mathematics." In *Spotlight on Young Children and Math*, edited by Derry Koralek, 19–24. Washington, D.C.: National Association for the Education of Young Children.

Singer, Dorothy G., Jerome L. Singer, Heidi D'Agnostino, and Raeka DeLong. 2009. "Children's Pastimes and Play in Sixteen Nations: Is Free-Play Declining?" *American Journal of Play* 1, no. 3 (Winter): 283–312.

Smith, Cynthia Leitich. 2000. *Jingle Dancer*. New York: HarperCollins.

Stojic, Manya. 2002. *Hello World! Greetings in 42 Languages around the Globe*. New York: Cartwheel Books.

UNESCO. 1995 Convention on the Rights of the Child.

———. 1996. "Learning the Treasure Within." Report to UNESCO by the International Commission on Education for the Twenty-First Century. Paris: UNESCO.

———. 1996. "Universal Declaration of Linguistic Rights." World Conference on Linguistic Rights. UNESCO. www.unesco.org/cpp/uk/declarations/linguistic.pdf.

———. 2008. *The Contribution of Early Childhood Education to Sustainability*. Paris, UNESCO.

UNICEF. 2002. *A Life Like Mine: How Children Live around the World*. New York: DK Publishing.

Van Hout, I. C. 2011. *Beloved Burden: Baby-wearing around the World*. Amsterdam: Royal Tropical Institute.

Vygotsky, Lev S. 1978. *Mind in Society: The Development of Higher Psychological Processes*. Edited by Michael Cole, Vera John-Steiner, Sylvia Scribner, and Ellen Souberman. Cambridge, MA: Harvard University Press.

Watts, Ann, and Phygenia Young. 2007. *Language Arts and Literacy*. Clifton Park, NY: Thomson Delmar Learning.

Wenger, Etienne. 1998. *Communities of Practice: Learning, Meaning, and Identity*. Cambridge: Cambridge University Press.

Whittaker, Jessica. 2014. "Good Thinking! Fostering Children's Reasoning and Problem Solving." *Young Children* 69, no. 3 (July): 80–89.

Williams, Karen Lynn. 1991. *Galimoto*. New York: Harper Collins.

Woodhead, Martin. 2006. *Changing Perspectives on Early Childhood: Theory, Research and Policy*. Paris: UNESCO.

York, Stacey. 2016. *Roots and Wings: Affirming Culture and Preventing Bias in Early Childhood*. Revised ed. St. Paul, MN: Redleaf Press.

With loose parts, the possibilities are endless.

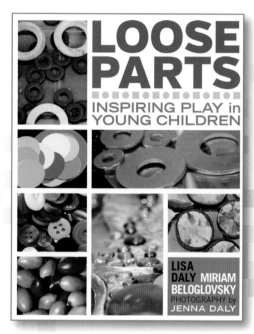

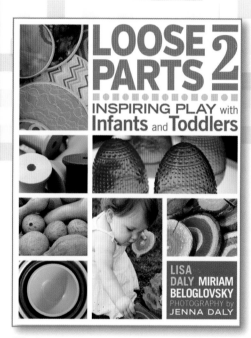